Loyalty Unleashed

PIT BULLS AND THE PEOPLE WHO LOVE THEM

Sue Torres

A portion of proceeds from this book will be donated to organizations that promote pit bull adoption, awareness and education.

ISBN: 1496133501
ISBN 13: 9781496133502

To my family – both human and canine

"The love we give away is the only love we keep."

~Elbert Hubbard

"I looked at all the caged animals…the cast-offs of human society. I saw in their eyes love and hope, fear and dread, sadness and betrayal. And I was angry.

'God,' I said, 'this is terrible! Why don't you do something?'

God was silent for a moment and then He spoke softly.

'I have done something…

I created you.'"

~Jim Willis

TABLE OF CONTENTS

FOREWORD

It all began in the fall of 2009 with an email from a total stranger who needed a printer. I had joined a free-cycle group in my town and a woman who was part of a local dog rescue was requesting a printer to make fliers for the dogs that were available for adoption. I had an extra printer that I was happy to pass along and, after meeting her, decided to browse the rescue's website.

A few weeks later I was volunteering at a rescue sponsored adoption event. I don't know if any dogs were adopted that day but my eyes were opened to a world I never knew existed. I knew about shelters. I had adopted my dog from a shelter. But rescue was different. I wanted to become more involved, but this particular rescue was just getting off the ground and there was not much I could do to help. So, I just took my newfound knowledge and went on with my life.

I joined Facebook around the same time, mostly so I could follow my daughter during her semester abroad. I could not have predicted how deeply these two events would converge to completely change my life.

I am not sure how it happened but one day I was alerted to the Urgent Part 2 Facebook page that posts daily "To Be Destroyed" lists of dogs in the New York City shelters. Here I saw an opportunity to save lives by networking the at-risk dogs and trying to help interested parties by directing them to the appropriate resources.

Of course, in order to network the dogs, I had to look at their pictures and read their stories. Of course I wanted to save them all, and of course, I could not. I had never thought about owning a pit bull, but the vast majority of the dogs I was seeing were pit bulls, and, one day I saw one that spoke to me named Augustine. I decided it was time to stop hiding behind the computer and actually do something. I decided I would foster him.

I was told by other people on Augustine's page about different rescues in the New York City area that I would need to contact for help and I filled out some foster applications, and while all this was going on, Augustine was rescued. I was happy and also relieved— did I really want to bring a dog into my home without even meeting him first? It all ended well for Augustine but now I was hooked.

I started learning the who's who of New York rescues. Over time I began attending events in the city and putting faces with the names I had seen online. I began volunteering with some of the groups by doing home visits with potential foster and adoptive families in nearby Connecticut, where I live, and helping to transport rescue dogs to their foster or adoptive homes. I was invited to join a special Facebook group of like-minded animal lovers who would network the death row dogs every night. It was on Facebook that I found my first pit bull.

Because of one dog that unexpectedly came into my life, I have met many wonderful people that I am proud to call my friends. I have found my passion and my reason for getting out of bed each morning.

Pit bulls have become my favorite breed. I am humbled by the depth of their love, devotion and loyalty. I have become their advocate and their voice, and as you will see, I am not alone.

THE PRAYER OF A PIT BULL

Spirit in the sky, who watches over all animals: It is my prayer and my request that you grant greater understanding, and acceptance to humans; those who love us, and those who hate us. That they will know how loyal we are, how brave we are, and how loving we are.

Help them to accept us as a breed in whole, and not let the few tragedies shine brighter than the many great traits that we have. To those who would kill me, let them know, I forgive them, even though I don't understand their hatred. To those who would beat me, let them know I still love them, even though it is not the honorable way. Thank you for all the strong traits that you have given to me, and my breed. Help those to know that I stand for courage, strength, loyalty, and bravery. And as my master already knows, let those who would come against my family know that I would surely die defending them.

And just one last thing that I would ask: Let my master know, that if you should call me away, that I will wait patiently at those Pearly Gates until the one who chose me, comes home.

Amen.

~Author Unknown

INTRODUCTION

"In the '70s they blamed Dobermans, in the '80s they blamed German Shepherds, and in the '90s they blamed Rottweilers. Now they blame the Pit Bull. When will they blame the humans?" ~ Cesar Milan

A lot of people, including many who love dogs, hear the term "pit bull" and visualize images of ferocious dogs that attack, maim and even kill. The media has been relentless with sensational stories of random attacks. Some states have even legislated against people owning pit bulls and certain other breeds.

How much is truth and how much is hysteria? Do we only hear the bad and none of the good when it comes to these dogs? What exactly is a pit bull? Hopefully these questions and others will be answered and you will come away with a better understanding of what it means to be a pit bull and what it means to own one.

Pit Bulls and Pit Bull mixes average about 38% of shelter intakes nationally, but in large cities the numbers are as high as 40%-60%. About 75% of municipal shelters euthanize Pit Bulls immediately upon intake, without them ever having any chance at adoption. Those that are offered for adoption are usually the first chosen for euthanasia when overcrowding forces the shelter's hand and decisions have to be made.

Studies estimate that up to 1 million Pits are euthanized per year, or 2,800 per day. Some estimates are up to double that number. In the Los Angeles area alone, 200 per day are put to sleep. A study by the organization Animal People reports a ninety-three percent euthanasia rate for Pit Bulls and only 1 in 600 Pits finding a forever home. (1)

We have all heard about aggressive pit bull-type dogs being used for nefarious purposes such as guarding, fighting and attacking, but what is less publicized is that pit bulls are also therapy dogs, police dogs and companion pets.

We hear the stories about pit bull attacks, and when one does occur, the headlines, without fail (and often erroneously), identify the attacking dog as a pit bull. If, on the other hand, another breed of dog happens to attack a human, the breed is not identified. When a pit bull, or any dog that resembles a pit bull, does something bad, regardless of the circumstances surrounding the incident, we are all made aware of the breed involved. However, when a pit bull becomes a seeing-eye dog for his blind brother and the two peacefully sleep in each other's arms, there is no mention of them being pit bulls – then they are just dogs. (3) We always hear the negative, but it seems like pit bulls do not get credit for heroism, loyalty, resilience and forgiveness, in the face of seemingly insurmountable odds. I guess that just is not sensational enough.

Strangely though, it was not always this way.

Did you know for example, that Helen Keller owned a pit bull?

Did you know that America's most-decorated war dog was a pit bull? Found as a stray near the military training grounds in New Haven CT, Stubby served 18 months during World War I. Participated in 17 battles, saved his entire regiment from mustard gas attacks, helped tend to wounded soldiers, and singlehandedly, caught and held an enemy spy. He earned the rank of Sergeant, and now has a place in the Price of Freedom exhibit at the Smithsonian. (2)

Remember the television show, "Our Gang" with The Little Rascals? Their dog Petey was a pit bull.

Around the turn of the 20th century, and for many years thereafter, pit bulls were used as "nanny dogs." They were entrusted to watch children due to their friendliness and loyalty.

So, that leaves us to wonder, what changed and why?

Over the past 20 to 30 years, due to their size and strength, through no fault of their own, pit bulls have become the dog of choice for guarding property, irresponsible breeding, and of course, dog fighting. Dog fighting has become a major source of income for criminals and drug dealers. Pit bulls are used for fighting because they are loyal and eager to please their owners even though, for the most part, they are gentle by nature. Actually, the vast majority of these dogs will not fight. These are the ones who are often used as bait dogs, abandoned, discarded or simply killed by their owners who deem them failures.

Too many of the pit bulls losing their lives in our nation's shelters, are there because they had the misfortune of being owned by people who are part of this culture. Many of these dogs have lived their lives on chains, resulting in frustration and pent up energy which can cause them to become aggressive. Still, as you will see, with love and patience, some of the most abused and neglected of these dogs can be family pets. Those reared from puppyhood in nurturing homes, are overwhelmingly loving, devoted and trustworthy.

When I decided to take on this project, I began by reaching out to the people I know who own pit bulls, volunteer in shelters or work in rescue. I also reached out to a friend, Theodora DeBarbieri, who writes a pet column for The Examiner. Unbeknownst to me, she published an article about a Connecticut woman (that would be me) who was looking for positive pit bull stories. The response was overwhelming and it was then that I knew I had to see this project through—for all the wonderful pit bulls out there and their very special humans.

The stories you are about to read are real. Some are graphic, others heartbreaking. The sad truth: abuse, neglect and animal cruelty are real and must be acknowledged. Many of the stories, however, are just about ordinary people and ordinary dogs that happen to be pit bulls. What all of these stories have in common is that all are uplifting and show the true nature of these amazing dogs, which turns out to be rather extraordinary, as you will see.

Hopefully, along the way, someone, somewhere will come away with a newfound appreciation for pit bulls and slowly but surely, perceptions will be changed one person at a time. Maybe after reading this book, someone who walks into a shelter to adopt a dog will stop at the cage of a lonely, abandoned pit bull and see him or her in a different light—and perhaps give a dog, which would otherwise have had no chance, a home. At least that is my hope.

1. http://www.examiner.com/article/pit-bulls-and-euthanasia-rates

2. http://amhistory.si.edu/militaryhistory/collection/object. asp?ID=15

3. http://www.today.com/pet shelter-dogs-caught-cuddling-are-adopted-after-outpouring-support-2D11644674

MY DOGS

When I look back on my childhood, for as long as I can remember, I wanted a dog. My brother and I begged our parents but our mom was adamant—no dogs. So we settled for stuffed animals and playing with our neighbors' dogs. I promised myself that when I had my own house I would have a dog.

It was at age twenty-six that I bought my first house. I could not wait to go to the shelter and pick out my very first dog. It did not happen quite that way, though. The young man that lived in the house had recently found a puppy under his car. He named her Emily. His family was moving out of state and he was going off to college. He begged me to take her or he would have to bring her to the shelter. So I did.

Emily was some sort of Spaniel, Beagle, and Border Collie mix, as far as I could tell. She was with me for the next sixteen years, through relationships, layoffs, career changes, a marriage, the birth of two children and a move to a new house. She was my best friend through good times and bad and she never judged me for any of the stupid things I did in my younger days. She loved me no matter what. It was with a broken heart that we said good-bye to her at the age of sixteen and a half.

Emily had been the perfect first dog. She loved everyone and everyone loved her. Even my mother, who never wanted a dog, became very fond of her. Emily's whole world changed when my babies were born, but she took it in stride and taught them the love that one can only learn from a dog. We had no plans on getting another dog because we already had the best—until about a year later when we went to the shelter to simply look at the dogs and wound up coming home with an eight-month old German Shepherd/Husky named Oscar.

Even though he was really still a puppy, we were already Oscar's third home. Why this sweet, gentle dog had been surrendered to the shelter not once, but twice in his young life, I will never know or understand, but he definitely chose us as his family. He jumped excitedly in his kennel when we stopped to see him and ignored others who displayed any interest—at least that is how we remember it.

He was energetic, yes, but he was a beautiful, kind soul, inside and out. He was patient when my daughter made clothes for him and dressed him up, or on another occasion, when my son hooked him up to a sled and had Oscar pull him around the yard. He loved the winters and the snow. Some of my fondest memories of Oscar were of him playing snow football with my kids and taking him sledding with us during a snowstorm on Christmas Eve. It was as if he knew that we were meant to be his family. He loved us for giving him a home and proved it in everything he did.

Oscar spent the next fourteen years with us. He saw me through a divorce, and both of my kids through college. At some point we noticed he was limping a little and our vet could not diagnose with certainty what was wrong with him. He kept getting worse though, and for the last two years of his life he was unable to walk on his own at all. We took him to physical therapy, gave him special vi-tamins and finally bought him a cart and some boots for his back feet. Some of my neighbors, who I had never met in almost 20 years, came out of their houses to meet Oscar (and me) when he cruised the neighborhood in his wheels. He touched everyone he met with his gentle nature, courage and resilience.

We can truly learn a lot from our dogs. They can teach us so much about devotion, determination and bravery in the face of adver-sity if we only pay attention. The most important lessons I learned from Oscar were to face life's challenges without complaining, to make the best of every situation and to be grateful for each new day.

In those last two years of Oscar's life, I became aware of the plight of dogs in the New York City shelter system. There were too many dogs, not enough homes and dogs were being killed at an alarming rate for routine illnesses such as kennel cough. The overwhelming majority of them were pit bulls.

I had never had more than one dog at a time and Oscar needed special care. The thought of adopting another was a little over-whelming, so I thought I would consider fostering. It would not be permanent and it would save a life. I could handle it. Then I saw a pit bull named Mickey and everything changed.

MY HAPPY TAILS

"Until one has loved an animal, a part of one's soul remains un-awakened." - Anatole France

There is nothing more rewarding than saving a life. It takes many people collaborating, each doing his or her part. For anyone wishing to volunteer, there is always something to do and no job is too small. While I am always looking for ways do even more, I do what I can to help save the lives of dogs that might otherwise have no chance. My involvement, though, is usually marginal.

I go on my computer every chance I get to network the dogs in need of homes. I am frequently asked by rescues to do home checks with potential foster and adoptive families. Doing these things does help, but I never actually have the opportunity to meet the dogs. I also transport dogs en route to their new families, but at that point, the dogs have already been rescued and are out of the shelters.

Every once in a while though, I get a chance to not only meet the dogs, but also to help them find homes and see them to safety. These are the times when I feel I am truly making a difference.

Clancy and Magnolia are two of my favorite "happy tails." My own dog Mickey is another. Here are their stories.

"The best and most beautiful things in this world cannot be seen or even heard, but must be felt with the heart." ~ Helen Keller

MICKEY
How the dog nobody wanted became the dog that changed my life

As I was looking through a Facebook page of at-risk dogs in New York one day early in 2011, there was one dog that stood out. He was a hound mix and I am a sucker for hounds. Something about their ears, I think. As I read this dog's biography, it was mentioned that he was surrendered to the shelter with another big white dog. The hound was adopted rather quickly and a few days later his canine brother showed up on the urgent list.

Mickey was, they said, a three year old pit bull mix. The shelter had conducted a behavioral test on him and he received less than stellar marks. He was very tense and anxious. Even the owner who surrendered him said he was "not too friendly".

Along with a group of other networkers (including the woman who had adopted his brother), I tried valiantly for days to find someone who would foster or adopt him. I am not quite sure why, but there was something about this particular dog that I could not get out of my mind. I found myself checking multiple times a day to see if he had been rescued. I pledged to donate money to any rescue that would save him. I contacted one organization after another, asking if they would take him. No takers.

Finally out of desperation, I offered to foster but I still could not convince a rescue to help. I was inexperienced with behavioral issues and there were red flags when it came to his temperament. I contacted every rescue I could think of and every one turned me down. There was also another problem. I had upcoming travel plans that could not be changed. Even if I went to New York to get him myself, I could not bring this dog home and then turn around and leave him a few days later. Things seemed hopeless, and to make matters worse, the shelter diagnosed him with kennel cough. His time was up.

I found my hero and Mickey's savior in the wee hours of the morning on the day he was to be destroyed, when I received a message from one of the rescues I had contacted previously. The Rescue Director told me she would help me as long as I agreed to adopt him – her rescue did not have money to fund his foster care. At that point I did not care what the conditions were as long as he was rescued. She told me she would call in and reserve him for me, and asked me to call her the next morning so we could talk.

And so I did. Just as I took a leap of faith with Mickey, this woman took a leap of faith with me. She only asked me not to divulge her name or the name of her rescue on Facebook because she was not able to do this for everyone who wanted to save a dog. For some reason though, she had a good feeling about me. She told me she would get him out of the shelter to the safety of a private boarding kennel where I would pay for his care and he would remain until I was able to bring him home.

That was a Thursday. I was not leaving for my trip until the following week, so on Saturday, February 12, 2011, my daughter and I took a ride to the kennel in New York to meet our new dog. He came bounding out, tail wagging and attempted to jump in our laps. He ate treats, went for a walk with us and played with the toys we had brought for him.

Meeting Mickey – February 12, 2011

The kennel manager said he already seemed like a different, much happier dog since leaving the shelter. And if he was sick at the shelter, he showed no signs of it only two days later, which led me to wonder if he had ever been sick at all, but that is something I will never know. Not friendly? Obviously there had been a mistake – he was great. We left feeling very good, especially knowing we had most likely saved his life. I could not wait to get him home.

Unfortunately things are often not as simple as we think, and two additional weeks in a kennel with thirty-five other barking dogs may have been too much for a sensitive dog. But, when he finally came home, something was different about Mickey.

I was told by the person who transported him not to pet him on the head because he was very fearful but he came into the house to meet Oscar. The introductions went off without a hitch. He came right up on the couch with me, put his head on my lap and took a nap. Everything was fine, just as I knew it would be, except all really was not fine.

Mickey was comfortable with me but he was clearly terrified of every other person on the planet. He would cower in fear on walks, tail tucked between his legs, posture slumped and he looked at me pleadingly as if to say, "Do we really have to do this?" He was afraid to even go to the bathroom outside. He would wait until we got back in the house. I was the only person he would allow to handle him, lunging, growling and snapping at everyone else that came near him. The woman from the rescue called me every day to check on us. She was incredibly supportive and tried to help as much as she could, but even she began to have some doubts.

Almost universally, people told me he would never be a suitable family pet and that I was going to have to make the tough decision before he hurt someone and the decision was taken out of my hands. I was heartbroken but I did have to consider the safety of my family, friends and neighbors. I thought about it but I just could not do it. He clearly loved me and I had fallen hopelessly in love with him. It seemed like love was something he had never had in his life. I just would not let him down.

I hired a trainer to find out what I needed to do. I had no idea if this would work, but I was going to try. Ultimately, if he failed to improve, at least I would know I did everything I could for him. Things started to get a little better. In a few days he was completely housebroken. He would only go in my yard at first but that was ok. After several weeks he had enough confidence to do his business on our walks. He learned to walk beside me on the leash, for the most part without pulling. It took some time and a lot of patience, but he did it. It took him quite a while, several months actually, to sit and stay consistently on command. We kept working on it though, and finally he figured it out.

Over time he learned to love and trust. I learned how to introduce him to new people and other dogs, and when introduced in a way that he would not feel threatened, he loved everyone. Now, once he knows someone he is a friend for life. It was not easy and there were a lot of bumps in the road and setbacks along the way. Some of my neighbors still turn away in fear because they remember how he was, (and, I am sure because he is a pit bull) but he has turned out to be the sweetest, most loving dog I have ever had. It is now difficult to imagine life without Mickey.

Most importantly, Mickey has shown me the ability to forgive and the true meaning of unconditional love. Because of him I try even harder to save more dogs like him, the lonely, unloved shelter pit bulls that only need someone to believe in them and give them a chance. I truly feel like I have found a way to make a difference and hopefully make this world a little better place.

An unwanted pit bull, dumped in a kill shelter and scheduled to die, opened my heart and changed my life in ways I could never have imagined.

Thank you Mickey. I am a much better person because of you.

CLANCY
It took a village

THANKS TO FOSTER MOM, LIZ, ADOPTIVE DAD, ADAM,
REBOUND HOUNDS RESCUE AND EVERYONE ELSE THAT
HELPED SAVE CLANCY'S LIFE

I became a volunteer for one of New York City's New Hope rescues, Zani's Furry Friends, after emailing the Rescue Director to ask her to help a would-be foster save a dog from death row. I am not always persistent, but when it comes to dogs I become a completely different person. I contacted the director over and over. I just knew she thought I was crazy! I was surprised when she actually seemed impressed by it. She jokingly said I must be part pit bull myself because I never gave up. We started an ongoing communication and developed a relationship. At some point she asked me if I would be willing to assist the rescue by doing home visits for potential foster and adoptive homes in Connecticut. I was delighted to help.

I also became acquainted by telephone with one of the other volunteers for Zani's Furry Friends. One day, the Saturday after Thanksgiving in 2011, we decided we would finally meet in person at the Brooklyn, New York shelter. I arrived before she did and met two of the amazing volunteers that devote countless hours to the shelter dogs. While we were waiting I joined the volunteers as they took the dogs for walks. Finally, my new friend arrived and we were allowed into the adoptions section of the shelter.

Now, mind you, I do not like to visit shelters anywhere or any time. I cannot bear to look into those cages and see those hopeful faces, knowing I am unable to take every single one of them home. That November day was no exception. I watched as my fellow volunteer walked around, took pictures of the dogs and spoke to staff members, and I tried not to fall in love with each and every dog I saw.

It did not work – at least not with one dog I saw that day. As I stood by his kennel he began clowning around, tossing his bed around and playing with his food dish. I said to my friend, "I like this one" and she said, "I do too." His name was Clancy.

We concluded our business at the shelter and headed into Manhattan for a fundraising event. I had not planned to attend but I had a wonderful time and met a number of people I only knew through my computer. All in all it was a great day.

When I got home I decided I was going to make it my mission to find Clancy a good home. I found him online and began networking him over and over again. I watched every day and cried every time I came across one of the dogs I had seen that day in the shelter, so full of life, in the "Gone But Not Forgotten" folder. The only thing that kept me going was that Clancy was still alive.

Clancy remained at the shelter. He survived a bout of kennel cough which is usually a death sentence, but for whatever reason, Clancy was spared. Every day I checked and watched to see if anyone was interested. Everyone seemed to like him but there were no takers. I noticed a woman from another rescue commenting on his page and I reached out to her. We became a tag team. She looked for people in New York and I looked in Connecticut. We had a couple of inquiries but nothing panned out.

For three months Clancy stayed at the shelter. It is almost unheard of for a dog to remain at the shelter for that length of time, but Clancy continued to defy the odds. Then one day he was adopted. All of us who had been watching him and trying to help get him celebrated and cried tears of joy. Our work had paid off – Clancy had a home.

Two days later however, he was back at the shelter. His adopter said he was too hyper. Three months in a cage and suddenly being thrown into a new home with strangers will do that, but some people will bail at the first sign of trouble and this adopter did.

Clancy was back and we kept trying but by then, life in a cage and maybe a taste of freedom, only to be locked up again had taken its toll. Clancy had become difficult to walk on a leash and had begun to guard his food. He was out of time and I was on vacation in Florida. I could not even go get him. Under any other circumstances, I would have.

Then, on Clancy's last night, a young woman named Liz appeared, seemingly out of nowhere, and wanted to foster him. By now though, some of the rescues were concerned about his behavior. I remember being at the airport on my way home and trying frantically to contact people from my phone in an effort to help Liz get her foster application approved by a rescue. It was touch and go, but finally it all came together. I credit Liz for never giving up and doing whatever was necessary to ensure that Clancy made it out alive. Clancy would be saved thanks to Liz and Rebound Hounds Rescue. He would have people that loved him and two other dogs to play with –Clancy had hit the jackpot!

Clancy went to his foster home and seemed to fit right in. Liz worked tirelessly with him on his manners and took him for long walks in the park and playtime in the yard. All it took was a patient, loving person to give Clancy what he needed. Liz and her family saved Clancy's life but still, they wanted him to have a home where he would be the top dog. Liz brought him to adoption events, bought him an "Adopt Me" vest and showed him off in her neighborhood and, along with Rebound Hounds, continued to search for a permanent home for Clancy. He had his own Facebook page where other people could help with the search as well.

It took months but finally Clancy was adopted and now he is home to stay. Between the time he entered the shelter and the time he was adopted, almost a year had passed, but now his new Dad, Adam and he are inseparable. If you happen to be in Central Park, you might see Adam rollerblading with Clancy running by his side. When people on the streets approach and admire this stunning, friendly dog and ask what breed he is, Adam is proud to say he is a pit bull.

In rescue it is often said that it takes a village. Thanks to a lot of people who worked together to save this sweet dog, he has his happily ever after.

I made many friends because of Clancy. The shelter volunteers, rescue volunteers, his foster family and his new Dad are all people

I remain in contact with to this day. Clancy was one of the lucky ones. He was given time when many dogs that enter the shelter system are not. Still we have to celebrate our happy endings when we can get them. For me, none makes me happier than this one.

MAGNOLIA
The long journey home

THANKS TO ADOPTIVE MOM EMILY AND
SMILING DOG FARMS ANIMAL SANCTUARY

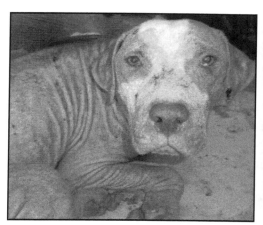

Magnolia 2009   *Magnolia 2013*

My friend Melody is the adoption coordinator for Smiling Dog Farms Animal Sanctuary in Texas. Not every dog that comes to Smiling Dog Farms will ever be adopted but is a remarkable place that accepts dogs from rescues, shelters and private owners. Many have been deemed unadoptable because of temperament, medical issues or old age. According to the sanctuary's website, "if a dog is breathing, he qualifies to come live here." At Smiling Dog Farms these dogs will be cared for and will have a home for the remainder of their lives.

One day Melody asked me to do a home visit with a family in Connecticut. This family wanted to adopt a pit bull dog from Smiling Dog Farms. The dog's name was Magnolia.

I read Magnolia's biography. She had been found emaciated, unable to stand and covered in Mange and bleeding sores. The incredible, caring staff at Smiling Dog Farms had taken her in and nursed her back to health. All the people who begged them to take her and offered to help eventually disappeared. Magnolia lived at the sanctuary for three years. Now it looked like she would finally have a home.

I was excited to meet the family that had chosen her – a young couple with a small daughter. I went for the home visit to meet them, so happy that Magnolia would finally have the life she deserved. When I met them, though, I had an uneasy feeling, although I did not know why. It was not anything they did or said in particular, that was wrong, it was just my gut telling me that this was not the right home for her. If any dog deserved a special home, Magnolia did, but this just did not feel right at all. I really hoped I was wrong.

I shared my concerns with Melody and although she also had some reservations, she spoke to the family at length and was assured that they were one hundred percent committed to giving Magnolia a loving, permanent home. It was decided. Magnolia would be transported to Connecticut from Texas.

I had hoped to meet the transport and see how the family reacted to her, thinking it would set my mind at ease but I was unable to do so on the day she arrived. A few days later Melody called to tell me that things were going well. What a relief!!

Sadly though, after less than a week, her adopters realized that Magnolia and their cat could not get along and decided she was not the right dog for them after all. They decided to give her back and Melody had to temporarily put her in a nearby boarding kennel. Magnolia immediately showed signs of stress, and her skin problems began to resurface. Melody told me that if a home was not found she would have no other choice than to send Magnolia back to Texas.

Then a miracle happened when I sent her pictures to a woman I knew named Emily! Emily is the neighbor of a woman I worked with that had recently lost her beloved dog. She had asked me to look for a puppy for her. Instead I sent her pictures of Magnolia. I was grasping at straws. Time was running out for Magnolia and here was someone who wanted a dog, but she wanted a puppy and Magnolia was already three. I was also not sure how she would feel about owning a pit bull.

Emily took one look at Magnolia and asked to meet her. Two days later I drove her to the boarding kennel and it was love at first sight. Emily took Magnolia home that same day. Magnolia is now living the good life. She has a big bed, clothes, toys, the best food and a family that loves her but her favorite spot is on the couch with Emily. I guess Magnolia was meant to come all the way from Texas to Connecticut so she could be where she truly belongs.

It was a long journey but Magnolia is finally home.

PART ONE

HEROES

"He is your friend, your partner, your defender, your dog.
You are his life, his love, his leader. He will be yours, faithful
and true, to the last beat of his heart. You owe it to him to
be worthy of such devotion."

~ Unknown

"You see, sometimes in life, the best thing for all that ails
you has fur and four legs."

~ Mark J. Asher

PIPER

THANKS TO LAURA BRUCCOLERI

I would love to tell about my four-year-old American Pit Bull Terrier, Piper. Piper is a Certified Therapy Dog, and serves as an ambassador in our state of Indiana.

Piper's therapy work is well beyond amazing. She spends a lot of time at an elementary school for Autistic children. With these children, she inspires them to read books and enjoy doing so. She has helped each and every one of them to feel compassion, trust, love, and patience. Piper also visits a children's hospital pediatric unit for cancer patients. Every visit she makes brings more and more smiles, and the entire staff welcomes her with loving arms.

Piper also hosts many advocate events such as the annual Coast to Coast Bully Walk, a global event, celebrated on National Pit Bull Awareness Day and the Peaceful Pit Bull Protest.

Piper was nominated for the American Hero Dog Awards in 2013 and placed ninth out of about thirty other Therapy Dogs. What an honor for both of us!

She has also been featured on Chicago, Illinois's local television station WCIU's "The U," and shortly thereafter was chosen as the station's "Top Dog!"

Piper was a special guest and threw out the first pitch of the 2013 season for Gary, Indiana's minor league baseball team, The South Shore RailCats. She has her own Facebook page, "Piper's Page of Life" with over twenty-five thousand fans. Piper is by far, my hero! She has changed so many minds, and has so much unconditional love in her heart for everyone she meets.

Piper is an example of her breed-not an exception. https://www.facebook.com/PipersPageOfLife

ATLAS

THANKS TO CHELSEY FLETCHER

Atlas is a rescued pit bull from Devore Shelter in Southern California—a high-kill shelter that acknowledges that ninety-five percent of pit bulls that end up there are put down due to a shortage of space, high intake, and low adoption. I was not looking for a dog. I had driven a friend to Devore to pull a dog to foster that she had seen online. While she walked away with no dog, I, on the other hand, left my heart there.

As we were leaving, an animal control officer walked in with Atlas, who at the time was only six months old, claiming someone on the side of the road handed him over on a leash, stating he was a stray. As such, he had a required five-day stray hold. I kneeled down to pet Atlas. He pushed his head into the belly of my daughter who was ten months old at the time, wiggling his butt into my lap. I knew I could not let him die there.

I visited him daily until he was able to be adopted, and I made it happen. To make sure he would not die, I planned to foster him until a home could be found. Atlas was pulled from the shelter on March 27, 2011. He was great in our home, goofy and wiggly. We had three other dogs at the time and he loved to play with them all. I had begun to notice a difference in Atlas though, he started limping; his feet turned strangely and kept turning. I noticed it at the shelter, but figured that maybe he had bulldog or basset hound in him (he seemed so small).

After a trip to the vet and a few x-rays later, we discovered he had a premature growth plate closure near his wrists which caused uneven growth of the ulna and radius. Cutting out the technical jargon, he required surgery or amputation to reduce the pain. One vet suggested euthanasia. After all, I would only need to replace the dog. Pit bulls are everywhere, was the notion. We spoke with a specialist and were quoted $5,000-$10,000 per leg to fix his problems. The specialist felt that correcting one leg would help his body correct the second on its own. We had to wait until Atlas matured enough physically to increase the chance for a successful surgery.

While we debated our options, as this was a large sum of money, we had our minds made up for us—by Atlas. I have struggled all my life with low blood pressure and heart issues resulting in fainting, though I have gotten pretty good at predicting and controlling those situations. One day, I collapsed in the kitchen. Atlas, at about nine months old then, left his toy behind and came to me. I woke a few seconds later with his head under my arm, waiting with me. When I was sitting up and fine again, he licked my face and went back to his toy.

It was also obvious that he and my daughter had bonded very deeply.

I immediately called my husband. Those two situations made up my mind—this dog clued into my "weak moment" and came to my aid when I needed him most. It was decided; Atlas was staying. Now, we had to figure out how to raise money.

I began baking dog treats and raised money through donations and treats to help pay for the surgery. We shipped about seven hundred pounds of treats in six months, raising about $4,000 in profits towards his surgery, paying the remainder out of pocket.

Atlas had his surgery on January 7, 2013. His cast came off a few months later, and the vet declared in July that he would not need the second surgery after all. He received his certificate of Canine Good Citizenship in March 2013, and was featured on the cover of a local military-base magazine as a winner of a contest on their page which advocates for bully breeds all over.

The journey to recovery was not a smooth one, due to the amount of pain Atlas was in on a regular basis. He developed fear-based/pain-based reactive aggression towards our other dogs. We had to work a lot on training after he was no longer on bed rest from his surgery. My husband talked about wanting to put him down, and I was called a bad mother for keeping him around. However, he is now a very sound member of our pack and he loves people as he always has. His bond with my daughter has remained unshaken through everything.

Every morning, he steps up and lays his head on her bed to greet her good morning. He runs to her and lies beside her if she cries. He still can sense when my blood pressure is low and will not leave my side. He will lay his head over my shoulder and nuzzle into my neck or cling to my side. He is a wonderful dog, eager to please, and deeply bonded and loyal to my daughter, myself, and now the other dogs in our home. https://www.facebook.com/AtlasTreatsForLegs

WALTER

THANKS TO LYNN READY ASPIOTES

We adopted Walter in the summer of 2011 from a shelter in Ohio. He was abandoned in the streets when a humane officer got a call to pick him up from someone's porch. I drove out and met him and when I learned how great he was with other dogs and with my dogs, we brought him home. Walter is very hard of hearing and is nearly deaf. Despite this challenge, within just three short months, he was certified as a Canine Good Citizen and Therapy Dog with Therapy Dogs International. Walter had quickly become a local star.

He keeps a full schedule and us very busy, visiting many places on a regular basis including local libraries, elementary schools, and events for the Western Pennsylvania Humane Society where I volunteer. Over the holidays, we will spend time at the Mall at

Robinson where volunteers wrap presents for donations to the shelter. Walter puts on a holiday sweater or collar and helps collect the money. He is wonderful with kids and even babies!

Walter also visits a local assisted living facility, Country Meadows. The residents pet him and love him and really enjoy when he visits. There are two other sweet, senior pit bulls, that were rescued by two friends of mine and they also serve as therapy dogs—Nola and Adora. The three dogs make their visits together sometimes, and I joke that they are his girlfriends. He gets so excited when he sees them!

Walter has brought much joy, love, and happiness to our lives and to the lives of countless others too. We love him so very much and we are so thrilled that we found him. Our vet estimated at the time that he was somewhere around ten years old. We hope he will be around for a few more years. We just cannot imagine our lives without this handsome old man. We hope that Walter shows everyone that old dogs can learn new tricks and that you can adopt an old dog from a shelter and have a wonderful family pet. https://www.facebook.com/walter.ready.5?fref=ts

TATORTOT

THANKS TO CHRISTI SMITH

I have been an approved foster for Ruff Start Rescue in Princeton, Minnesota for a little over three years. I have seen some of the worst things and some of the greatest things through this rescue. I have also met and made some of the greatest friends anyone could ever ask for! I have given countless hours, conducted many home visits, processed many applications, donated money and supplies, and have fostered a ton of dogs. Who would have guessed my pit bull foster would save me from the worst heartbreak in the world by saving my son!

TatorTot was pulled from Minneapolis Animal Care and Control (MACC) by Ruff Start Rescue. He was originally supposed to be a foster-to-adopt situation. After months of trying to make him a good fit for a family, things did not work out as planned and he came back to the rescue.

I had seen another dog I wanted to pull from MACC, but the timing was not right. Once again, I had been informed about TatorTot, known back then as Gator, (a stupid name if you ask me). At first, I thought he was going to be at too high a level of energy for my family, and that he would just end up stir crazy. Boy was I wrong!

I picked up TatorTot on Saturday, September 28, 2013. My first reaction was, "Oh my, what a strong boy!" I then took him home, let him play in the yard, fed him, and took him to the pet store for some new items, like a collar, leash, food, chew toys, and training treats. When I got home we immediately went to work on training. He knew "Sit" and "Shake" right off the bat, and I thought to myself, "This is a good start!" I have since taught him more leash manners, as he loves to pull. I taught him to go lay down when we are having dinner. I also taught him to sit and wait for his food until I give him the OK. Little did I know that he would become my medical alert dog!

On Wednesday, October 2, 2013, I put my son to bed about 8:30 p.m. as usual. It always takes a few tries to get him to actually go to bed, so I waited a bit until he was asleep before going to bed myself. At 1:30 a.m. my son came to me, acting kind of strangely—nothing to be concerned about, more like he was deliriously tired. So off he went, back to bed. I did not realize it right away, but my foster dog TatorTot (a brown/red Pit Bull Terrier) was starting to act strangely too. Before I knew it TatorTot was running back and forth between my son's and my room, barking and whining. I told him to knock it off and tried to get him to come lay down with me. Finally, after making the correlation that something was a bit off with my son and TatorTot's behavior, I went to check on my son. He was completely out. It was not a heavy sleep, he was unconscious, but not like any other passed out child. TatorTot was still barking and whining and licking my son's face. Any other child surely would have awakened. Even when I was trying to wake him, he remained motionless. As I scooped my son in my arms, I whispered, "Good boy TatorTot!"

I then rushed my son to the hospital, finding out, after countless hours in the emergency room, that his glucose levels were dangerously low. They ran some tests thinking it was Diabetes type II. They gave me supplies and taught me how to administer glucose. They also told me to go see our Pediatrician right away. After checking his levels every couple of hours (without being on medication) everything looked normal again that day. We went to the doctor and had tests run. On October 4, 2013 we got the tests back. My son's results were negative for diabetes! We still have not discovered the root cause, but this was a good start.

As for my handsome TatorTot, he is my saving grace. He is the most well behaved pit bull I have ever met. I owe everything to this wonderful dog. He saved me from the most heart breaking pain any mother could feel. Without his help, I could have lost my son. My pit bull saved him! How do you honestly repay a dog for saving a life and saving you from heartbreak? I knew that night, laying in that hospital with my son, presupposing what might have been, the only thing I could do (besides spoil the heck out of him) was to adopt him! Later that morning when we got back, I emailed the rescue, because another family wanted to meet him again. I told them what had happened and they agreed he should stay.

My story went viral on the internet among the rescue community. I have received an overabundance of love and support. I have even had people offer to pay for his adoption! Now, if anyone wishes to make a donation, I request that it go towards training for TatorTot to become a therapy dog, or to Ruff Start Rescue so they can save more lives. I am truly blessed to have a wonderful son, an amazing pit bull, outstanding friends and family, a small but powerful rescue, and the love and support from the rescue community. I owe all of my gratitude, love, and protection to my pit bull TatorTot! https://www.facebook.com/tatortotthepitbull

BLUEBERRY

THANKS TO MAURA PORTER

Blueberry was surrendered to the Milton Animal League (MAL) by her owners who thought she had Mange. She actually has allergies. When she came into the shelter she had bright red skin and had lost a lot of fur. Under those harsh conditions, Blueberry had recently delivered a litter of eleven puppies. Her previous owners, prior to MAL's involvement, had her living in a laundry room. The family was selling her puppies for money, so she was essentially just part of a backyard breeder's plan. When they did not want to spend money to clear up her Mange, they surrendered her to Milton Animal League. It was a great day for me. I volunteered there and had recently lost my dog to leukemia. Beth, from the Milton Animal League, had re-named this dog Blueberry and so the name was kept, as it is perfect for her, and home she came.

A long-standing wish was to become involved in therapy dog work. However, my previous dogs were not a good fit for this opportunity. Given her history of being bred and kept in a small space, I really did not know if Blueberry would like visiting with people. If she was dog aggressive or if there were any other situations which, given her past would not make her a good candidate, time would tell. The good news: my concerns were unfounded, as Blueberry has succeeded in every aspect of her training and in the therapy dog world.

We started off by training for the American Kennel Club (AKC) Canine Good Citizen test. She was the first dog to pass in her group. Next, we signed up for therapy dog training through Dog B.O.N.E.S. (Building Opportunities Nurturing Emotional Support) of Massachusetts and again she passed with flying colors. We have been doing therapy dog work for almost three years now and recently she was awarded the AKC Therapy Dog certification as well.

Blueberry is a natural therapy dog. She is caring and loving with great compassion. We visit nursing homes, rehab hospitals and colleges during exam times. We have also visited those affected by the 2013 Boston Marathon bombing. We have been assigned hospice patients who we visit weekly, and visit with blind and deaf residents of the New England Homes for the Deaf. She brings more joy to people than I could ever have imagined. What is amazing to see is that her breed does not matter to the people with whom she visits. All they see is her love. And that, to me, is perfect beyond words.

Here are a few favorite stories:

November 22, 2011: During today's visit to the New England Homes for the Deaf (NEHD), we had two great experiences. First, a gentleman—who I was later told never engaged in conversation, avoided all eye contact and stayed to himself—came into the office and signed that he wanted to meet "the dog." During his time with Blueberry, he smiled. The staff was floored by his interaction, as it had never occurred before. Then later we met a woman, Jayne, who works at NEHD who was very, very fearful of pit bulls. Blueberry did what Blueberry does and, at the end of our visit, Jayne stated that she loved Blueberry, and thought she was "gentle, kind, and gave great kisses." I know I have said this before, but I couldn't be prouder of Blueberry. What a great visit today.

February 9, 2012: Today's therapy dog visit started off with Blueberry finally getting the rehab hospital's receptionist (who had said for months that she was petrified of pit bulls) to sit and spend some time with her. But really the highlight was meeting a woman in the lobby who came to visit her mother. The woman asked if Blueberry was a pit bull and was amazed (her word) when I responded that she is. After telling me of her mother's love for dogs, I told her that we would go right up and pay her a visit. When we entered the room, I lifted Blueberry up on the bed and her mother broke into a wide smile and stared, saying over and over, "A dog, a dog, a beautiful dog."

We were there for quite a while. When we left, the daughter told me, with tears in her eyes, and I quote: "You have no idea what Blueberry's visit did for my mother, today. She loves dogs so much and Blueberry has just given her more joy than she had had in a very long time. Thank you, thank you, thank you!" Yes, thank you Blueberry.

July 13, 2012: Today Blueberry and I were accepted into a local hospice pet therapy program—and Blueberry is the first pit bull ever to be accepted into this hospice's pet therapy program! I am hopeful that now that the door has been opened, many more pitties or pibbles (or dogs that just look like they are) will be accepted. I am so proud of my Blueberry girl!

October 8, 2012: Today was our first hospice visit. Unfortunately the woman was really too sick to be able to respond to Blueberry. However we had a wonderful interaction with a family that made the day worthwhile. As we were going down in the elevator, a woman and her three young children were inside. I could tell the mother was nervous about Blueberry. As we were leaving the building, I overheard the woman telling her children that therapy dogs help people. The same woman approached us, remarking how her daughter saw Blueberry as more than a dog. In her estimation, Blueberry was a superhero because she helps others.

Then the mother asked, "Excuse me, but is she a pit bull?" When I said yes, she said, "I am petrified of pit bulls, they scare me so much. I never thought they could be therapy dogs." I told her that she was just about to have her first positive pit bull experience. I had Blueberry sit and I spent the next few moments telling her and her children about pit bulls and about Blueberry. I then gave a bone to the youngest child, a girl who was three-and-a-half years old, and told her that Blueberry was a gentle eater and that she could give the bone to her.

The girl did, successfully, and all of a sudden Blueberry was being petted by three sets of young hands ranging from three-and-a-half to six years old. You could see the once apprehensive look on the mother's face change from disbelief to jubilance at seeing such a tender display between the dog and young children. The mother began petting her too! This was truly a wonderful transformation. As we left, the mother expressed thanks and I overheard the three-and-a-half-year-old say, "Mommy, I really liked that dog." My Blueberry is a superhero indeed!

December 11, 2013: Blueberry has been under the weather but since she was feeling better today and since it is the last time we will visit this particular facility before Christmas, we wanted to make our scheduled rounds. We spent time with the usual suspects who light up when they look around and see Blueberry enter the room. I wish I could bottle that moment of recognition and the emotions emitted at that moment. It's beyond precious. We did have a few new patients. One woman was quietly petting her when she said, "I don't even like dogs that much, but I would take her home with me." Our last new patient was a woman from Vietnam who did not speak English, but she spoke the language of loving dogs beautifully. She softly touched Blueberry's head, ears, neck and body. The smile never once left her face. When we gathered up to leave her room, we looked back at her and she was waving to us and still smiling.

Blueberry is now helping other dogs gain their Canine Good Citizen certification through Clear Skies Dog Training and is also a TV star. Blueberry and I recently went into Boston and were filmed and interviewed for "About Health TV" with Jeanne Blake, the award-winning talk show medical reporter. Sometimes it is just about that one person who might never have been near a pit bull before. It's about reaching over that barrier just for a moment and in that brief instant—all I have to do is let Blueberry be Blueberry. https://www.facebook.com/pages/Blueberry-the-Pit-Bull-Therapy-Dog-Changing-Minds-One-Visit-at-a-Time/218206764888576

ECHO DOPPLER

THANKS TO CAREY YARUSS SANDERS

This is the story of Echo Doppler, miracle dog.

I adopted Echo from the Massachusetts Society for the Prevention of Cruelty to Animals (MSPCA) in Boston in the spring of 1999. I was fresh out of college and working at Angell Memorial Animal Hospital, which was connected to the MSPCA.

On my breaks I would regularly go down to the MSPCA shelter to play with the abandoned puppies before they were put up for adoption. One day, I was delighted to find a litter of six pit bull mix pups that desperately needed baths. They had been found in a parked car covered in their own feces and urine, severely malnourished and neglected. Luckily, police officers broke the car windows and took the pups to MSPCA where they would have a chance at new lives. Soon all six found new homes and I figured I had seen them for the last time.

A few weeks later, I learned that one of the puppies had been brought back when his family discovered he had a heart murmur. Further tests showed that the heart murmur was serious and he most likely had irreversible heart disease. It was suggested he be put to sleep.

Although I was told that he probably would not live to see his second birthday, I had become attached to him and decided to adopt him myself and show him love for whatever time he had. I named him Echo Doppler as a reminder of his disease so that I would be forced to keep things in perspective. Seven months later, to the amazement of the cardiologist, his heart murmur was nearly gone–and without any medication or surgery. Someone I met said that his heart was too full of love to have left any room for disease, and I would have to agree.

He became best friends with my roommate's cat, who also suffered from heart disease and was rescued from the same shelter. It was almost as if they knew.

I discovered Echo's uncanny ability to sense trouble a few months later, when I took him to the park. We were about a mile into the woods when we saw a horse with no saddle galloping by. Echo took off like lightning in the opposite direction. I ran after him but quickly lost sight of him. I started to cry, thinking I had lost him for good. Then I heard howling. Echo had never howled before but I was pretty sure it was him.

Eventually I saw him about 50 yards away, frozen in a sit-stay position. I called him but he wouldn't budge. When I got closer I saw the rider who had been thrown from the horse. Echo then jumped up, wagging his tail to greet me.

As it turned out, the rider was afraid of dogs and yelled at me to call my dog off, not realizing that Echo had just rescued him. Echo and I ran a mile back to the car to call an ambulance. The man didn't even thank us but the EMT's told Echo he deserved a medal for bravery.

After that, I was convinced that Echo would make a wonderful therapy dog. He was certified as an MSPCA Animal Assisted Therapy Dog and also earned his Canine Good Citizen badge. We started at the Hebrew Rehabilitation Center for the Aged, where he would visit with people living there in the nursing home or in hospice. Then we moved to New York City, and we went to a soup kitchen, once weekly, to visit with the people who came there for their meals.

There were always people who would hear what breed he was and shudder, but as soon as they met him, he would change their minds. Surprisingly, I found that the older generation in the nursing homes didn't have the breed prejudice that the younger generations had. He was so well trained and behaved really well in the nursing homes, but the one thing I could never "fix" was that he thought all of the tennis balls that the residents had attached to the legs of their walkers were for him and he would dive for them. He seemed to know that once his sickness was gone, his heart had extra room for people who really needed big hugs and wet pit bull kisses.

Echo provided ten years of service with me and was also a canine blood donor who saved many other dogs in need of transfusion. He was photographed for Garry Gross's book "Beautiful

Old Dogs" that came out on November 2013, published by St. Martin's Press.

A lot of my friends and family were very wary about pit bulls when I first adopted him. So many of them have now come around and have either adopted pits of their own, or at the very least, become advocates for the breed. I adopted my second pit, Figment, last January.

ABRAM

THANKS TO ELIZABETH

I have always been a dog lover. Aussie/Catahoula, German Shepard, Labs—I loved them all. My dog Sugar was attacked by a pit bull twice. I did not hold it against the breed really, just the person who neglected the dog. Then I met my boyfriend Joe, who incidentally, wanted a dog. He did not want just any dog - he wanted a pit bull. I really had no qualms about this, but I knew nothing about the breed. So this started me on my research journey. Next, I found a dog needing a home, but when we went to pick him up, we found a totally different scenario. There were two-pound puppies! Weaned! I was shocked! But I grabbed a puppy and ran when the owners said any puppies left after the weekend would probably be used for fighting. After leaving, I found out that they not only were weaned early, they were just four weeks old! We named our puppy Abram.

Fast forward almost two years later. In that timeframe, I had trained Abe myself to be a mobility service dog. He is a stellar dog with a sweet demeanor and great friends with my ten year old cat. Now, I am starting a service dog training service for veterans in Vermont. I plan to use rescue pit bulls when I can. What better way to honor our veterans and save lives at the same time!

TESS AND KANE
Paying it forward

THANKS TO KIM GEORGE AND KANE'S KRUSADE

I have always had a passion for animals and those in need. Tess was the first pit bull dog I adopted about four years ago. Two years ago I adopted Kane from a shelter outside of New York City. He was on the kill list – which means a shelter euthanizes for space, unfortunately. They thought something was wrong with him but he was just depressed. He was definitely abused and fearful. He had to be taught how to live in a house, play with toys and go on walks. It has been wonderful to watch him discover what it is like to be a dog.

Two weeks after I got Kane, Tess was diagnosed with Mast Cell Tumors. It is systemic and surgery is not an option. She has been on chemotherapy for two-and-a-half years. She has a great quality of life with zero side effects. I refinanced my home to lower my mortgage payment, so I could absorb the monthly $200 chemotherapy bill. I was very grateful that I could afford to save her life, but it started me to thinking about what people have to do when they cannot afford to care for their dogs. This was a major inspiration for Kane's Krusade. The other inspiration was the discrimination I experienced as a pit bull dog owner.

I wanted to hold Kane and Tess up as "Ambass-a-bulls" to show people that pit bull dogs are just dogs. Kane is a Certified CGC (Canine Good Citizen). He is American Staffordshire Terrier and American Bulldog with Basenji, Bull Terrier and Scotty thrown in. Tess has not had her DNA screening done yet.

Kane's Krusade is an all-volunteer 501(c) 3 non-profit organization in Springfield, Massachusetts. We improve the quality of a dog's life in two ways: through the distribution of (C.A.R.E.), Canine Assistance, Resources and Empowerment kits. Kits are assembled and passed out by our volunteer C.A.R.E. Krew, who in turn, spread awareness via organized campaigns to educate and demystify falsehoods regarding pit breeds. This results in keeping beloved dogs in their homes, out of shelters and off the streets. We are not a dog rescue—however we do network with several area shelters and rescue groups.

We were incorporated in the state of Massachusetts on March 28, 2012, becoming a 501(c) 3 on June 8, 2013. It only took us eight weeks which is almost unheard of! We have about thirty-five regular volunteers called "Krew" members. We also have on average, another fifty, who come together for special events like our Dog House Build Off. Despite not having a salaried staff, we currently provide C.A.R.E Kits to twenty-three families and forty-seven dogs. This means, every three weeks, we make home care visits providing dog food, toys, treats, etc. Other pet needs being met: spay and neuter services, medical care, vaccinations, microchips and grooming to our families' dogs. We also have a Krew member providing in-home behavioral training to families.

Our medical fund treats minor ailments like skin issues, ear infections and dental work. This funding also affords us opportunities to care for dogs in need of minor surgery. We do not perform cancer treatments or orthopedics because we just do not have the funds right now. We spend about $1200.00 from our medical fund each month. We also provide a respectful and humane end of life for dogs who are suffering. So what this means is, we will fund euthanasia and cremation services, which have been provided for two dogs so far, and are about to be offered to a third, who is seventeen years old.

We build long-term relationships with our families in a non-judgmental way. This results in keeping loved dogs with their families and preventing economic surrender of dogs to shelters. We have partnerships with the Thomas J. O'Connor Animal Control Officers, Dakin Humane Society and the Second Chance Animal Shelter and Wellness Center. These partnerships enable us to keep costs as low as possible.

We work in the poorest neighborhoods in Western Massachusetts. These neighborhoods are known as "pet care deserts." Dog owners have no access to veterinarians. There are no pet food stores in these areas, oftentimes not even grocery stores. There are no shelters. Providing proper nutrition and preventative care, let alone emergency care, is practically impossible. Most of the families we work with do not have cars. When their dogs get sick, they cannot bring them to a vet in a taxi or on a bus, even if they could afford it. Most of our families do not have computers or smartphones. We serve dog owners whom no one else is reaching.

These are the dogs and the owners who are falling through the cracks. We go right into their homes, bringing resources, information and opportunity to them where they live. We form long lasting relationships of good will and trust. We have a "pay it forward" policy, meaning: we provide a hand up- not a hand out. After six months of services, we require our families to give back to our organization in one of six different ways—whatever feels comfortable to them. This can be anything from providing a written or video testimonial, paying for a portion of their dog's food each month, helping us build dog houses or becoming one of our volunteers, lending a helping hand to other families in need of the same services they themselves benefitted from.

Dogs eat an average of 15-20 pounds of dry food every three weeks. On average, we go through about 700 pounds of dog food every three weeks. Even without adding any more families, we would deliver over 12,000 pounds of dog food in our C.A.R.E. Kits annually. However, we add about two to four new families every month. To date, we have yet to turn anyone away. Most of our food and treats are donated. We provide leashes, collars, Sense-ation harnesses and name tags. In addition, we build customized and insulated dog houses called Kondos–which basically have two rooms.

One is the entrance/hallway and the other is a "bedroom"– separated by an insulated wind wall, stuffing the Kondos with straw for added warmth. We provide heated water buckets as well and provide kennels and fences when possible, although this is not the main function of the group. We will do whatever is necessary to get a dog off a chain. The first goal is to work with the owner in getting the dog inside safely, away from harsh weather, etc.

In 2014, the goal is to launch our first Community Dog Day, which will provide spay/neuter vouchers, free shots, exams and microchips right here in a Springfield Massachusetts neighborhood. Our highly anticipated launch efforts for January 2014 have begun for the *Krusader Klub, which is a monthly donor program with special perks. *(http://www.kaneskrusade.org/blog)

We believe love knows no color, age or breed. Dogs are individuals and should be judged by their actions, not their breed. We believe every dog has a right to a safe, happy life, free of chains and suffering. We believe in doing what we can to ease the suffering of dogs, and raise their quality of life. We will not turn anyone away and we will advocate for each and every one, every day.

Simply put, we keep families together, one dog at a time. We stress the following: you can either judge or you can help a dog. You cannot do both.

Do not let perfect be the enemy of good. https://www.facebook.com/JoinKanesKrusade?ref=br_tf

MAC

THANKS TO ROCHELLE STEFFEN

I would like to tell you about my rescued pit bull Mac. He has literally donated thousands of dollars from his grass roots campaign on his own Facebook page—almost $10,000 in 2013. He has changed so many lives, dogs and humans alike, over the past year. We were contacted a few months ago by a woman who follows his positive-only Facebook page, who said he kept her from killing herself with his silly and upbeat page. That moved us profoundly. It does not get much more positive than that! Not bad for a dog we bought off a corner from some questionable folks, to save him from being mistreated. By the way, he weighed four pounds at three months old when we got him in April 2011.

He has become a special needs guy with his own struggles of multiple surgeries but still has an amazing way of moving the world from his couch. At eight or nine months of age I knew he had issues with his back legs. After many different vet visits and an array of therapies and treatments, surgery was the only option. November 21, 2011, was his first surgery at the University of Missouri Teaching Vet Hospital in Columbia. To date, he has braved through four surgeries on his first bad leg with over nine months in a crate due to numerous complications. Eventually, he will need his other leg operated on for the same genetic defect. Mac is Pit Bull Strong and uses his positive energy to help others even while dealing with lots of his own ailments. Mac raises money for other pit bulls in need by selling t-shirts and car decals/stickers through his Etsy store. "I Am Pit Bull Strong" is his trademarked way to give back. One hundred percent of any money raised from his shirts/decals go towards "Mac's Fund", for other pit bulls that need a forever home.

Mac has a loving home and wants to pay it forward so others can have loving homes like his.

We are in the process of becoming a 501(c) 3 to help him grow his "pay it forward" campaigns. His campaigns include $100.00 donations to pit bull rescues. He is giving away $1000.00 on his Facebook page currently and we are nearing the $10,000.00 mark. Mac does a monthly doggie goodie box for dogs dealing with huge health issues, abuse, cancer, etc. He also has an Amazon wish list that shares his toy/treat donations with his local dogs at the shelter. Mac and his other siblings foster sick and injured dogs and we help our shelter by getting them treated and adopted through his page. A family recently drove from North Carolina to adopt a Labrador puppy we found dumped with a broken leg. Mac's Facebook page got the donations for treatment for this puppy, who might not have survived otherwise. Mac is truly a hero! https://www.facebook.com/macthepitbull

LUCKY

THANKS TO STACY HALLMAN

Lucky is a seven-year-old American Pit Bull Terrier. Her life started out horribly on May 5, 2006. My ex-husband and I had helped a neighbor save her dog's litter of puppies. Lucky had somehow managed to get wrapped into a pool tarp, practically all day in the hot Alabama heat. She survived and we were able to take her home. Now mind you, I was convinced that pit bulls were horrible and that they attacked for no reason. I did not want Lucky but I also did not want to see her sent to the shelter. I decided to put my fears aside for this little puppy who had survived all odds.

Almost a year to the day, my ex-husband and I divorced and I took Lucky to live with me. During the divorce proceedings I lost custody of my son. So there I was, after ten years of marriage, single again at Christmas time, with a dog that I still really did not care about. So many nights I would lay awake crying for my son because he was no longer living with me and I literally had no friends. During those nights, Lucky would cuddle up next to me and just look at me like she knew what I was going through.

As the months went on and I had no heat, Lucky proved to be my very own personal heating blanket and emotional support. There were so many times I just wanted to give up and end my own life, but as I would start to go down that horrible path, there was Lucky to bring me back to the present with her calm nature and loving ways. Now mind you, when Lucky was left alone she loved to destroy anything that she could get her mouth on from remote controls to couches and everything in between. But each night that

I would come home feeling down in the dumps, she was there to brighten my night and just be there for me.

Now fast forward a few years and now my son has come back to live with me. Heartbreakingly, I had discovered that all had not gone well with his last living arrangement. There was Lucky to step in and take over the role of emotional support. Many times my son would sit in his room so quietly and I would look in to find Lucky curled up next to him with her head on his lap looking at him with a look that just said I know what you are going through and I am here for you. Lucky helped heal my son to a point where he can function and not focus on his past.

Lucky got extremely sick almost two years ago and I almost lost her. I remember kneeling in front of her while she was lying on the couch, crying and begging her not to leave me, that my life would not be the same without her. Funny how I went from not wanting this pit bull because of negative stereotypes to having my heart ripped out because I thought she was dying. I am happy to say Lucky pulled through and now seven years later, she is the most loving pit bull you will ever want to meet.

Lucky is my best friend, she will show you her eyes to let you know that she understands what you are going through and that she is there for you. I dread the day she crosses the Rainbow Bridge, but until that day, she will be my best friend and my confidante. I love my Lucky to the moon and back!

BIGGIE

THANKS TO NICOLE MILLETT

My dog was found on the streets of Sacramento. He was in pretty bad shape too. He was saved by an amazing and brave woman who could see past his scars and his breed. She instantly knew he had suffered and saw a scared creature in need of help. Over the next few months she took care of having him neutered and vaccinated. She struggled to find a home for him since pit bulls are not the most desired dogs and he did show deep signs of aggression, (we suspect he was used for fighting) and behavior, so he certainly was going to be a challenge for someone.

I have suffered from chronic depression since I was a child, and fell into several abusive relationships that left me very damaged and broken. I had a few plans to commit suicide, but never went through with them because each time, at the last minute I realized I wanted to live. I knew I could not go on this way so I thought maybe a dog would make me feel like someone loved me. Maybe this is what I needed to help me cope with the loneliness and would stop the feelings of dread I experienced every day I was alive.

I had a new focus-almost daily I would look at rescue websites. I probably browsed through hundreds of photos, but remained pessimistic through the whole search. Anyone who has lived with depression knows that it is very difficult to transition into feelings of hope or positivity. I have never experienced anything like the love at first sight emotion until I saw my dog's photo. I saw him on a courtesy posting on a rescue site, and I knew from the second I saw his photo that this dog was meant to be mine.

I knew I needed to get in contact with the woman who was taking care of him. I needed to meet him. When I inquired about him at the rescue, the person running it told me he was not available, and that I should probably look at a different dog. I am a pretty determined individual, and was not about to take no for an answer. So I found the name of the woman who had the dog, and I Google searched her like a crazy stalker and found a phone number. When I called, she sounded a bit surprised, but very excited at the thought of a potential home for this adorable guy!

We set up a day for me to come over to her house and meet "Mr. Big," as she had named him. I was pretty nervous as I drove over to her house. What if he did not like me? I rang the doorbell and as soon as it opened, this stocky angel-faced dog trotted over to the door to greet me. So trusting and so gently, he rolled over on his back to get a belly rub from me. The bond was instantaneous, I had to fight tears. For the first time in such a long time, I felt pure joy and love. This was my dog. Since adopting Mr. Big, now named Biggie, my quality of life has improved more than I could have ever imagined or hoped for.

I have worked with him a lot so that the previous behaviors have been curbed. Biggie is trained to the point that he is no longer anxious or aggressive towards other dogs. He is a sharp boy and a very quick learner. He is so relaxed and easy going that he even nibbles and sucks on a blanket before he goes to sleep! I think he just needed to find some stability just like I did. He has taught me that everyone deserves a chance to be trusted, and no matter what your past holds, that is not what defines you as a person. You can let go of your past because the future can be bright - if you let it.

Biggie reminds me to forgive and to love unconditionally. He makes me laugh every single day just by being his goofy self. Even when I have a horrible day and feel like giving up, he is right there by my side to reassure me that I am not alone.

When I cry, he will curl up next to me and lick my face to try and make me feel better. I work as a veterinary assistant, and he is honestly the sweetest dog I have ever met. The stigma around pit bulls is such a silly thing to me. People judge me because I have tattoos, piercings, and colored hair. People judge him because he was born a pit bull and has cropped ears. When we are out walking together, people probably think some pretty off the wall things about us.

We have experienced people crossing over to the other side of the street when they see us coming. Some have grabbed their children by their arms and pulled them away from us. Other experiences have seen us being yelled at, making horrible statements or telling me my dog should be banned or euthanized. I used to get very angry, but I have learned to laugh and brush it off when people take a look at us and automatically think we are dangerous or delinquents. All I know is that they are really missing out on having two great friends. I just wish people could try to open their minds and their hearts and accept these wonderful dogs as what they truly are—sweet, snuggly, oversized lap dogs.

I truly believe that if I had never adopted him, I may not be here today to talk about it.

LILY DUCHESS

THANKS TO KRISTY LOVE-NELEIGH

My rescue American Pit Bull Terrier is a Mobility Service Dog in Texas. She also has a Canine Good Citizen (CGC) title.

Lily Duchess was taken from drug dealers. She has burn marks on her body. She weighed only fifteen pounds when she came into my life. The beautiful girl is my Service Dog. She goes to church with me. The kids love her. Being that she was one of the first pit bull service dogs in Texas, people are amazed by her. We have changed so many minds on pit bulls in San Antonio and other areas we have been in Texas.

You truly would be amazed at how sweet this fifty-seven pound, pure love, pit bull is. Lily would like people to know she is thankful for being able to snuggle and spend time with her human family and her fur sister Coco Princess, who is an American Kennel Club Registered Therapy Dog. She is also thankful that she can help to teach people that pit bulls are great dogs. https://www.facebook.com/pages/Lily-Duchess-Pit-Bull-Service-Dog/441433202610218

DOMINIC

THANKS TO DAN ENGLAND – GREELY (CO) TRIBUNE

The city of Denver has a pit bull ban which is strictly enforced. While animal welfare organizations believe such legislation is simply a knee-jerk reaction to a small number of isolated incidents, to be born a pit bull in the city of Denver amounts to a death sentence in many cases.

Dominic and his siblings had the misfortune of being born in Denver. They were seized as puppies by police during a raid and taken to a shelter. If they were not moved out of the city quickly they would have been destroyed. Luckily for them, they wound up at the Denkai Community Veterinary Clinic in Eaton, Colorado, where they would have a chance to be adopted.

Vet tech, Stephany Haswell offered to foster two of the puppies and brought them to her home in nearby Milliken, which she shares with her husband, three children and three large dogs. She immediately told her children "no" when they begged to keep the adorable puppies.

Haswell carefully screened anyone interested in adopting the puppies to make sure they went to loving homes. By the time the process was completed, her neighbor decided to adopt one of .puppies and her family had fallen in love with the other, a little gray one with bright blue eyes that they named Dominic. He was named after the Vin Diesel character from *The Fast and the Furious* movies. Since he fit right in with the family's other dogs, he quickly became a welcomed addition.

Being just a puppy, Dominic seemed to always be underfoot at home so Stephany brought him to work with her. It was there that she discovered Dominic's amazing gift.

One day a dog who had just come out of surgery, was placed on Dominic's big red bed. Dominic immediately went over to cuddle up as if to comfort the dog. Even though he loved to cuddle with everyone at home, the people on staff at the clinic thought he might have just been cold. Later that same day, though, they changed their minds when Dominic did something quite remarkable. He went over to a pile of dogs, who after surgery, were whimpering and crying. As if sensing their pain, he cuddled up to comfort them where they had lain. He seemed to instinctively know which dogs needed him the most and gave them the most attention.

Now Dominic has a job at the clinic. He even has a title – Denkai Recovery Specialist. When a dog is in surgery, Dominic waits at the door until the dog comes out. Then he goes to work. Dogs coming out of surgery can be confused and sometimes wild, but with

Dominic there to comfort them, they wake up rested and calm. Dominic does not discriminate at all - he cuddles with cats, too!

The workers at the clinic have never seen a dog quite like Dominic. They feel extremely fortunate to have this amazing little guy as part of the staff to provide comfort to the clinic's patients when it is needed the most.

LILLY

THANKS TO DAVID R. LANTEIGNE & MARIA ALVES

Just after midnight on May 3rd, the engineer of a westward-bound freight train witnessed an extraordinary scene as he barreled toward a railway crossing in Shirley, MA—a dog was frantically pulling an unconscious woman away from the tracks. The engineer made every attempt to stop the train but was unable to avoid striking eight-year-old pit bull Lilly before she could clear herself from the train's wheels.

Lilly's human companion was unharmed but the dog was not nearly as fortunate. The train's wheels sliced through her right foot, fractured her pelvis in multiple locations and caused other internal injuries. Critically wounded, Lilly lay down next to her companion, who remained unconscious until help arrived.

The train's engineer later told first responders that he witnessed the dog pulling the woman, Christine Spain of Shirley, off the tracks as the train drew near. Lilly's calm and composed demeanor—despite the wail of sirens, flashing lights and frantic din from first responders struggling to make sense of the scene, is all the more remarkable given her life-threatening injuries, which by now were bleeding profusely. A Shirley animal control officer immediately drove Lilly to an emergency animal hospital in Acton where Boston Police Officer David Lanteigne, who adopted the once shy and anxious dog five years ago from an animal shelter, recovered her and rushed to Angell Animal Medical Center in Boston.

David had adopted Lilly three years ago as a companion for Christine, his mother, who had suffered from alcoholism nearly her entire life. Upon arriving at Angell's Emergency and Critical Care Unit, Dr. Alice D'Amore immediately took charge of Lilly's care. The administration of sedatives and pain medicine calmed her enough to allow the veterinary team to determine the extent of her injuries, and plan for the emergency surgery and ongoing treatment she would require. Lilly's right foot had been completely "de-gloved"—its skin, muscle and connective tissue torn clear away. Multiple fractures to her left pelvis were especially troubling because, should she survive surgery, she could be permanently unable to bear weight or walk without assistance.

The veterinary team concluded that Lilly's right front leg could not be repaired and the only option would be to amputate the entire limb. Lilly braved the necessary surgery. Her life will never be the same as she will be unable to bear weight or walk without assistance for the first few months after her surgery. Still, the veterinary team at Angell is optimistic that the spirit she showed as she rescued Christine may be just the trait that sees her through this new phase of her life.

Lilly's selfless bravery has captured the hearts of the entire staff. Her injuries were very serious and her road to recovery will be long. But she has the character and spirit that sometimes trumps all of our medical advances when it comes to recovery. I think she's got what it takes to get back to her former self.

Because of the severity of Lilly's injuries and the extensive treatment she required, the MSPCA-Angell has provided financial aid through its Pet Care Assistance program to help cover the cost of Lilly's care. In addition to supporting other MSPCA programs, Pet Care Assistance provides financial aid to families whose animals need emergency, intermediate and critical care at Angell. Readers who would like to donate to Pet Care Assistance can navigate to www.mspca.org/helplilly.

At a time when pit bulls are maligned and erroneously stereotyped as violent or unfriendly, Lilly's bravery is testimony to the true nature of these amazing dogs. Far from being aggressive, unfriendly or indifferent, Lilly is a bona fide hero and an ambassador for pit bulls everywhere. The MSPCA-Angell's Advocacy, Law Enforcement and Adoption Center teams have worked for years to challenge the notion that pit bulls are innately dangerous. It is only recently that pit bulls have been cast erroneously as villains. At the height of the breed stature in the early 20th century they were often seen as the most decorated heroes in the U.S. Lilly has demonstrated the unconditional love and loyalty that is a hallmark of pit bulls—and many, many other dogs as well.

Said Jean Weber, the MSPCA's director of animal protection: "Lilly's story has moved us all beyond measure. I hope her actions will underscore the truth about pit bulls—that they are amazing animals and are as devoted to their family as any other dog."

Once Lilly fully recovers from her surgeries she will go home to live with David, his girlfriend and their two Golden Retrievers (whom Lilly adores). Christine has moved in with David to help with Lilly's convalescence. Lilly's recovery will be monitored regularly by the veterinary team at Angell to ensure she has every chance of returning to her former self. https://www.facebook.com/LillyTheHeroPitBull

PART TWO

TRIUMPH

"Life is an ever-flowing process and somewhere on the path some unpleasant things will pop up – it might leave a scar, but then life is flowing, and like running water, when it stops it grows stale. Go bravely on, my friend, because each experience teaches us a lesson. Keep blasting because life is such that sometimes it is nice and sometimes it is not."

~ Bruce Lee

"The seeds of great victory lie in minor triumphs."

~ Toyotomi Hideyoshi

VICTOR

THANKS TO MOM LINDA, MAKING OF MIRACLES STORIES (MOMS) RESCUE, CARAPATHIA PAWS AND ONE STEP CLOSER ANIMAL RESCUE (OSCAR)

My name is Victor. I came from a high kill shelter in Georgia. Meike Wilder from Carpathia Paws saw me in the shelter. I do not know what they were thinking, because I am obviously not a girl, but the shelter people labeled me "pregnant female" because I was so swollen from heartworm. Meike did not care what I looked like. She knew she loved me and was determined that I would live. She pulled me out of the shelter, got me to a doctor and began to look for a home for me.

My foster mom Linda heard that Meike had too many dogs in her home waiting to be adopted. She told Meike to send her someone, that she could foster one in New Jersey. Meike chose me! Making of Miracles Stories (MOMS) rescue drove down to Georgia, and brought back almost 30 dogs. I was one of them. My foster mom Linda drove to southern New Jersey and picked me up.

I was not neutered. X-rays showed stage 3 heartworm and many gunshot pellets. In addition, my hip and leg had been kicked repeatedly and smashed. I had numerous bite scars on my face and chest, but my foster mom thought I was beautiful. She made sure I got the very best care. Long-term heartworm treatment was started. I was neutered. Training began, and I met hundreds of people. I loved everyone! One Step Closer Animal Rescue (OSCAR) in New Jersey listed me and started looking for my forever home.

Expensive surgery was needed, and people—generous, caring people—responded. Funds for my surgery were collected, and we waited until my heartworm was better so I could be operated on.

Finally, my hip and leg were fixed, and some gunshot fragments (near nerves and causing a lot of pain) were removed. I was finally going to be able to run and play, just like all the other dogs! I had to take my heartworm medication for a year and a half but now I am heartworm free. It took months to heal from my surgery, and one leg will always be shorter than the rest—but I can now use all four legs!

My foster Mom Linda adopted me in January, 2013. I have my own Facebook page with over 11,000 fans. My Facebook page is called "Unlucky Victor" but I feel like the luckiest dog alive. https://www.facebook.com/pages/Unlucky-Victor/225822237446097

EDDIE JUSTICE

THANKS TO CLAUDIA STAUBER

My dog Eddie Justice is about eight years old. The short story is that he was found emaciated, with his skull bashed in and his jaw broken. Eventually his eye leaked out and could not be saved. It all sounds bad but he is one of the happiest dogs I have ever met and truly the best dog I have ever owned. He was adopted from a local rescue called Justice for Dogs.

Eddie is also the author of Eddie's Tails, a book written for dog lovers. Our goal is to inspire everyone to treat animals with love, kindness and compassion! It is no secret Eddie is an extremely talented writer. I still have not figured out how he types with those big paws and just one eye, but it does not surprise me. Eddie continues to amaze me every day! More of his story is also in his book and on www.eddiejustice.com.

I met Eddie on December 1st of 2012 and he has been well-fed, warm, and happy since that day. He lives in Morrisville, Vermont on 12 acres in a log cabin, where he is free to run around wherever he wants. He meets new friends all the time. He also goes on walks every day with different human and animal friends and is incredibly excited about that.

Eddie accompanies me for book signings and other rescue events and we have even been on the local television news. We decided that all the proceeds of his book will go to animal rescue so many other dogs will be as lucky as he is. Last, but not least, Eddie prefers convertibles to closed cars, at least in the summer. May all beings be happy! https://www.facebook.com/eddiejusticevt

TYKA

THANKS TO BETH CITURS

My husband and I have two German Shepherds and four cats, in addition to two children. We began fostering dogs through a local rescue here in Minnesota, called Secondhand Hounds (SHH). We tended to gravitate toward Shepherd mixes because we love them, but there was such a need for pit bull fosters that we decided to try and immediately fell in love. I never necessarily bought into the media hype but I always thought it was better to be safe than sorry—why not just get a different breed? Well that was before I got to know pit bulls.

They truly are the most affectionate, loving dogs I have ever met. When I watch the stories of soldiers coming home from overseas and seeing their dogs get super excited, it is heartwarming, but I get that kind of greeting from my pit bull every day when I get home from work!

My pittie, Tyka, was found wandering the streets of Minneapolis in January 2013 with literally no fur, and it is cold in Minnesota in January. She had Demodex mange that had gone untreated for so long that she lost almost all of her fur and was bleeding. Minneapolis Animal Care & Control (MACC) took her in and SHH immediately pulled her because she was a pit bull with mange—a combination that is usually a death sentence at MACC.

Another foster with SHH took her initially but then went on her honeymoon a week later, so we took Tyka temporarily until her foster parents came back. Well, by the time they did, we knew we wanted to foster Tyka until she found her forever home, so we kept her. It took a couple of months for her to get better and by the time she was adoptable we knew we could not give her up, so we adopted her! Tyka also recently became a TV star when she appeared on the news.

We are still very concerned over MACC's policies and a group of us are hoping to inspire change in regard to some of its policies with respect to pit bulls. We hope Tyka will change many lives, just as she has changed ours. https://www.facebook.com/TykasTale

JACKSON

THANKS TO JENNIFER THOMPSON

I must tell you about my boy Jackson! This comes from someone who was totally skeptical of the pit bull breed.

A friend of mine is involved with rescue groups in Greenville, South Carolina. It was last year, about mid-December, that my friend posted a picture on Facebook of a dog that had been found by someone she knew.

I saw the picture and my heart just broke. This dog was covered in scabs, blood and pus. It looked like he had gravel all over his body. His head was sort of sunken in and he was very skinny. It was hard to tell what kind of dog he was. He looked like he had some lab or boxer in him-that is what I wanted to believe.

I had recently moved back up toward the mountains and found a house with some land. The only thing that worried me was my two mini Dachshunds and how they would feel about a stranger in their home. I sent a message to the woman who had the dog, anyway. Her name was Caroline and she told me all about the dog she had named Max.

As we were talking, I told her that I was very interested in taking him in. She said there was a younger man that wanted him too. I think she could hear my tears on the other end of the phone and said, "I would much rather you have him." She said she was going to take him to the vet, then we would arrange a time for me to come get him.

Caroline called me later that day to give me the news about the vet visit. His mange was Demodex mange, which is not contagious. She did state some dreadful words, well, I thought so at the time anyway, that he was a pit bull. I was very apprehensive about this. I have always loved animals, I had a Rottweiler in college—another breed with a bad reputation—and he was the best dog I had ever owned.

Still, a pit bull to me was just scary, I will admit it. I could not possibly own a pit bull, could I? I told Caroline that I would take him but if he was aggressive with my two other dogs I would not be able to keep him. She understood and said that she would take him back and find him a home if it did not work out.

Caroline called me the next day, crying hysterically. Max had an adverse reaction to the medication he was taking. She was not sure if he was going to survive. He had tremors and would not eat or drink. She said she would keep an eye on him and hoped he would pull through. I sent her texts throughout the day to check on him. She called me the next day and said he seemed a little better. She was crying and said, "This boy wants to live."

Thankfully Max did indeed pull through, and Caroline brought him to my house on December 23, 2012, the day before Christmas Eve. She pulled up and he hopped out of the car wearing a striped sweater. The poor thing looked pitiful—he had absolutely no hair. We went inside and sat down on the floor in the family room and got to know one another. My two little dogs came out to meet him. Reese, my female, was fine with him but Gus, my male, was less welcoming.

It never phased Max one bit. He seemed fine around the smaller dogs. He actually got down on the ground to be at their level.

Scooted his little scabby self across the floor and reached his head out ever so gently to give them a sniff and a kiss with his tongue. Gus growled at him and Max backed away—scared of a 12-pound little Dachshund.

After that, Max just ignored the little dogs and focused more on Caroline and myself. He would dive on us head first and do silly headstands in our laps. He seemed to be very goofy and sweet. I promised Caroline I would do my best to give him a good home.

After she left I looked down by my side and there he was—Max, the pit bull. I had a pit bull in my house that I knew nothing about—nothing about where he came from or what kind of life he had lived. I had no idea if he had even been potty trained yet. Then I reminded myself about all of the homeless dogs and all of the abused dogs and all the dogs living in horrific conditions. It was my turn to actually contribute and help. It was, after all, Christmastime and I had the space and the time to at least make a difference in one dog's life.

I watched him sniffing around the family room. He would stop every once in a while and look up at me, wag his pink tail a little bit and then go back to sniffing. He eventually went to lie down on the hardwood floor. It made me sad that this poor guy was in such bad shape. I bought a nice big bed just for him and he chose to lie on the hard floor. Our estimation is that he had probably slept in worse places.

I kneeled down on the floor and crawled over to his bed and gently patted it and said, "Max come here, this is your bed, this is for you." He got up, walked over to me and cowered down. I think he was confused as to what the bed was and that he should lie on it. I encouraged him by patting the bed again and saying, "Come here and lay down." He took one of his paws and gently placed it on the bed and quickly got in it and curled up. I sat there and petted him for a little while. His poor skin was so cracked and scabby it was almost like petting sandpaper. I got back up and looked at him and it made my heart smile. There he was in a warm house, in a nice bed, next to a Christmas tree.

We had a bit of a challenge with Max, due to him not being able to take his medicine. We had to go a more natural route suggested by our vet, who hoped it would work for him. He was put on a grain free diet, with daily baths to help his skin heal. I got him lots of sweaters so he would not be cold outside and I had to rub him down with coconut oil daily so his skin would not get too dry. He was a real hit at the vet's office. Everyone seemed to just love him and he loved them right back with a face full of excitement and a constantly wagging tail.

I went on the internet and started to really research the breed and began to learn about the dreadful pit bull. I found that it was primarily the media that sensationalized these God awful stories about pit bull attacks. I learned that they are actually great dogs when owned by responsible owners and that they were known as nursery dogs back in the early 1900's because of their kind demeanor and gentle nature with children.

The more Max and I got to know one another, the more comfortable we felt with each other. I had to give him a bath every morning and he was such a good boy in that bathtub. After getting to know him I was not crazy about the name Max but I wanted to keep it similar. I thought of Jax and then Jackson and I knew immediately that was it. Jackson it was, a.k.a. Jack!

As time went on, his personality really started to shine, and what a sweet boy he is! He does not have a mean bone in his body. He loves everyone but he is still scared of Gus.

Jackson has healed completely. He still has a few scars but he is full of life and energy. He likes to chase deer and take long naps in front of the fire. His morning routine consists of getting one of his stuffed toys and bouncing around the family room with it, shaking his head and growling. He will do the occasional headstand on his bed with his body sideways over his head. He finishes the routine by rolling around on his back and letting out these crazy growling and moaning noises. He does this for a good five or ten minutes, then it's time for food and out the door to see what is going on outside.

He has become my favorite out of all my dogs. I look forward to coming home and seeing his happy face. He brings so much joy to my life and I would not trade him for the world. He is, hands down, the best dog ever! Now I will probably never own another breed. I'm very thankful that our paths crossed and even though people say I am an angel for rescuing him and making him healthy again, I'll tell you what—he rescued me right back.

PENELOPE

THANKS TO ALYSSA ELLMAN

At just eight months old, Sally (now named Penelope) found herself on death row at the Brooklyn, New York Animal Care Center. She was severely abused, neglected, starved and just waiting to die. She had been picked up on someone's front lawn in Queens, New York and was brought to a high-kill shelter.

In a tiny metal cage with no bed, blankets or love, she was 25 pounds and should have been at least 45 pounds. She was covered in giant open gashes that were all over her body, including the bottom of her feet. In her intake picture, her head hung low like she was defeated and had given up.

Since she was brought in as a stray, she sat there on a three-day stray hold with little or no medical attention. After three days, she was eligible to be pulled by a rescue and taken to the vet. She would not be transported to me in Boston for about four days, until she was feeling a little better. This poor baby was just a puppy.

When I picked her up, it broke my heart to see her still so emaciated and covered in sores. She jumped out of the van and gave me a hug and we have been together ever since. She is now around eleven-and-a-half-months old.

Penelope never held the torture she endured before she became a part of our family against anyone. She was our foster dog but I knew the second we got her that she was never leaving. Now she loves strangers, animals and especially children and is one special pit bull, touching many hearts including my own.

My girl Penelope has also changed the minds of many people who may have had negative thoughts about pit bulls. I am so proud of my girl, we love her so much. We foster a lot of dogs and recently, I bought a whole litter of four week old pit puppies that a homeless man was selling on the streets in Massachusetts. I am happy to say they are all safe and in loving homes now.

OLIVIA
(Formerly known as our little girl)

THANKS TO MOM LYNN TELLER AND
ST. LOUIS STRAY RESCUE

Olivia – October 2011

Olivia and brother Cabbage – April 2013

Looking at Olivia today, she is happy, healthy and so full of life. It is hard to imagine that her life began in a far different way.

On a Thursday, in the fall of 2011, St. Louis Stray Rescue responded to a call from the Citizen Service Bureau, a department within the city that handles resident complaints. On that day, a woman called to complain that her own two dogs were starving and dying in her basement. She wanted the city to remove the dogs.

By the time rescuers arrived, the woman had already thrown one of the dogs into a dumpster, thinking he was dead. The other dog was barely able to stand due to starvation. When they checked the dumpster, the rescue team found a male dog clinging to life. He was named Our Little Boy and his companion, Our Little Girl. Both dogs were rushed to the rescue's Trauma Center.

Sadly, the abuse suffered by Our Little Boy was too much for his little body and the doctors were unable to save him. Randy Grim, the rescue's founder had this to say at the time: "I doubt City Hall, the country, or other animal agencies have seen or understand the scope of animal abuse in St. Louis. We should be disgusted and disgraced at what we has happened and for what has been allowed to become a part of many people's daily lives, abuse to our four legged companion animals.

There is no support to change North St. Louis. There are no monetary or educational resources in place to reduce this growing issue. All we have is ourselves, those who truly care what happens, and to clean up the mess and shed tears over these deplorable outcomes. I live in an ignorant city."

Miraculously, though, Our Little Girl survived. Today she is known as Olivia, a beloved member of the Teller family, along with her pit bull brother and best friend, Cabbage.

The 22-year-old owner of the dogs was arrested and charged with abuse and neglect of her dogs. Her punishment? One year of unsupervised probation, 24 hours of community service, an animal care class and a $75 donation to the Humane Society of Missouri. The woman was prohibited from owning any animals while on probation, but expressed a desire to own another dog at a future date.

Since that time, the city of St. Louis has made significant progress in cases such as these with the formation of a Mayor's Task Force and The Stracks Fund Matching Gift Challenge, initiated by the Mary Lou Shanahan Foundation. Right now, if you donate to The Stracks Fund, which provides emergency medical care, the Foundation will match up to $135,000.

In the state of Missouri, however, those convicted of animal cruelty still usually receive a mere slap on the wrist. Even sadder is that two years ago nothing would have happened to the dogs' owner as prosecuting animal abuse cases is something very new in St. Louis.

This case, as much as any other, shows the need for stronger laws and stricter penalties in cases of animal cruelty and it cannot happen soon enough. Olivia is an amazing example of courage, resilience and the ability to forgive. We owe it to her, and so many others like her, to protect our companion animals from harm and advocate for change.

It is the least we can do.

BUDDY

THANKS TO LESLIE POLIAK

Two years ago, our beloved German Shepherd/Chow mix dog died of cancer. His name was Buddy and we had him for thirteen years.

Six months later, my daughter and I began thinking about adopting another dog. The last breed I ever thought of was a pit bull but nearly every shelter we went to had more than its fair share of the breed.

One day we landed at the East Valley Shelter in Los Angeles. We met a volunteer who showed us around. He particularly enjoyed my 24-year-old daughter who is high functioning autistic. The next day we went to more shelters but ended up back at the East Valley Shelter with the same volunteer. He led us to a cage with a dog cowering in it. He was so dark that we could barely see him.

The dog was a dark brown pit bull that had been brutalized and used as a bait dog. He was emaciated, had scars and open wounds all over his body and was afraid of everything. To my surprise, my daughter asked to go in the cage with the volunteer. I was afraid for her safety but let her go anyway.

Dakota (my daughter) fell in love with the dog. He had just been picked up on the street two days before we met him. What is interesting is that the shelter had named him Buddy, which she took as a sign.

We left the shelter and went home where we discussed adopting Buddy. My biggest fear was that we would adopt this dog and he would end up being aggressive with us, or that potential behavioral issues would cause friction with our cat and neighbors. The next day though, we called the shelter and let them know we wanted the dog.

Buddy had to be neutered and was on antibiotics for his open wounds but two days later, we brought him home. The volunteers at the shelter cried tears of joy when we left. Because this was all new to him, when we got him home Buddy was shy, tentative and scared but grateful for everything we did for him.

This dog has brought so much joy to our lives. He is a goofball, loves the cat and has formed warm, loving relationships with my daughter, myself and everyone who comes to the house. He is funny, loyal, protective, smart and extremely affectionate. He has no idea how big he is and will sit in your lap if you let him.

We love Buddy with all our hearts. He has touched us and everyone we know.

MOOSE

THANKS TO DANNY COMEAUX

My name is Danny Comeaux but everyone calls me DC. I spent most of my adult life partying and not taking care of my responsibilities, and three years ago I found myself in trouble with the law. I do not look at this as a bad thing, though. It was a wake-up call and I knew it was time to make some changes in my life.

I decided to take a negative and turn it into a positive. I have been around pit bulls most of my life. Moose, an American Staffordshire Terrier, came to me when I had hit rock bottom. I looked at him after getting him from a puppy farm and said, "Let's show the world we're not bad. We have love to give and we can prove it."

I am absolutely in love with pit bulls. They are amazing animals and I wanted to show my two sons, ages sixteen and nine, something positive. I hoped to teach them that they could start making a difference with animals and also with themselves. Moose and I started training to hike the Appalachian Trail. We trained for nine months. The trail is a two thousand one hundred and eighty six mile hike from Georgia to Maine. We started out on April 6, 2013, at Springer Mountain, Georgia and finished on September 5, 2013 at Katahdin, Maine.

We had to overcome many challenges; the heat, bugs, rain and injuries, but we did it. I said from the beginning that we started as a team and we would finish as a team. "We-Will-Finish" was our motto. Our Facebook page with the same name was started for friends and family, but it turned into something much, much bigger. We now have followers all over the world.

My goal is to raise awareness and bring an end to breed-specific legislation (BSL). I have now decided that we are going to attempt to conquer the Pacific Crest Trail in 2015 – which is two thousand six hundred and sixty miles of hiking from Mexico to Canada. Currently, the fastest time for completing it is 59 days. Our goal is to break the record. Moose and I will be training as well as spending time with my sons. I am trying to get my oldest to attempt the hike with us and to work promoting a positive image of pit bull dogs. I hope to show my boys that two negatives can create a positive world for dogs and people alike.

MIKO

THANKS TO DANNIE GABBERT

In late 2007, my friend told me of a three-month-old pit bull who needed a rescue. She was being sold for fighting. My friend was told that the puppy which had yet to be sold was starving. I said I would try to help find a home for this puppy. I personally did not want a pit. I guess deep down I was afraid of them though I knew better than to believe the hype.

Two weeks passed, the puppy still needed a home and I decided to take her, even though I had three other adult dogs. We had to get her when the person who was trying to sell her was gone. When we showed up, someone brought her out to us. She was three months old, weighed just 12 pounds, had been crated 24/7 and as a result she was caked in feces and urine to the point that she had developed burns.

Despite her living conditions and lack of human contact she was the happiest little thing I had ever seen! She was bouncy and full of kisses. She even had what I called happy feet, she literally danced when she got excited and still does. Saving her was one of the best decisions of my life. I love pit bulls now. My little girl's name is Miko and she is now six years old. My partner, who was so frightened of pits that she would not even come into my house unless I was home or even a glance at Miko, has since turned into a pit bull lover and advocate right along with me!

ALLIE

THANKS TO LISETTE CASTILLO

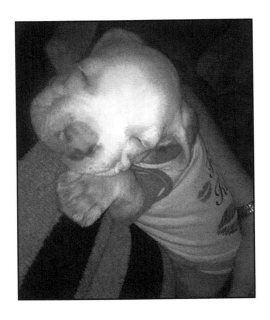

My family rescued our pit bull mix from Compton, California.

It was just after Valentine's Day in 2012. My son's godmother, Erika, called me. She was devastated and needed to vent. Erika's neighbor had a litter of pit bull puppies. She had four pit bull mixes herself and felt horrible that she could not do anything for these pups. She could see them through her back yard fence and hear their cries for hours. She told me the puppies were dying one by one. The parents were siblings and had been bred themselves and with previous siblings for dog fighting and sales. From so much breeding these new puppies were born too small or had something wrong with them. They were being left outside in the cold, hungry and not taken care of at all. Erika asked me to go over to her house to see if I could get someone to save them. She knew I lived in an apartment and it would be hard for me to raise a pit bull mix, as much as my family loved dogs and wanted to have one.

We had to do something. I asked Erika to go over to the neighbors and talk to them to see if they were willing to give them away to someone that could care for the pups that were left, instead of letting them die. The neighbors agreed but not without first collecting 80 dollars. I drove down a few hours later and before I arrived one more had died and only two were left.

Without a second thought and knowing I would probably have to move out of my apartment, I went ahead and gave the neighbor the 80 dollars and took one of the puppies. Although she already had her pitties, Erika decided she would help also.

I ended up going home with our approximately eight-week-old pup Allie. Her deformity was her tail. It is actually the cutest thing in the world at about five inches long and crooked. Erika went home with Sunny, who we later discovered was deaf.

My Allie got sick within the first week and ended up in the ER with a stomach infection and worms. From the very beginning she was full of love. So playful and using her mouth for everything– on the couch, shoes, our pants and hands.

Now that she is trained, she is not a barker, and gets along with other animals including cats and rabbits. She does not chew up shoes or the couch anymore. All she likes to do is sleep, play fetch, do tricks and sit at the window and look outside for hours at a time. Of course we had to invest a lot of time on daily walks, food, doggie parks, vet check-ups and training, but it was all worth it.

She is one happy, loving, outgoing, friendly girl. She stayed short in size, measuring around 17 inches tall and only 50 pounds, but is very healthy. By the way, I did not have to move. My neighbors got to know her and my building manager was also a dog lover and could tell Allie's temperament was great. We got very lucky!

Family, friends and kids love her and she loves them. My mother was terrified of the breed, because of all the media and news reports. She did not even realize that Allie was a pit bull until one day my sister mentioned it to her. My mother was in disbelief. Allie could not be a pit in her eyes–she was a nice doggy. It just goes to show that the media is not accurate!

Almost two years later, Sunny is doing great too. He gets along with the other pitties at Erika's house just fine and is living the life of a great dog with a huge backyard to run and play in. He also stayed small (about 45 pounds) but is a loveable dog and good with the kids and family too.

Since saving Allie's life, I encourage other people to adopt pit bulls, especially those that are at risk of being killed. I am proud to announce that I have been able to help save a few from dying. I love the breed and truly believe that with any breed, not just pit bulls, the dog's behavior is a reflection of the owner and the training and attention that is given–not the dog!

SEAMUS

THANKS TO CORRI JIMENEZ

In January 2010, I worked for the USDA Forest Service in the Sequoia National Forest in Dunlap, California. While I was working at my desk, I heard a dog whimpering—a sound you do not hear in the halls of a USFS ranger district. I got up from my computer and followed the whine, knocking on the door to one of my coworker's offices. On the floor was a four-month-old white pit bull puppy, shivering in a USFS jacket. He looked up at me with big brown mascara-like eyes and it was at that moment I wanted him. I petted his head, and repeatedly told him he was okay. My coworker, Carolyn, said he was found dodging cars at Sequoia Lake in over one foot of fresh fallen snow with a sibling (that unfortunately was never caught) and pulled into the comfort of a warm USFS vehicle.

Carolyn and other USFS personnel explained to me that they all had adopted dogs abandoned in the forest from Fresno and the California Central Valley. Seamus, a pit bull mix, was yet another victim. He was a little malnourished and had engorged ticks on his ears, something you would not find at an elevation of 5,000 feet in the Sequoia NF. "He doesn't have a home, Corri," said Carolyn. "You should take him - otherwise we have to take him to a vet hospital that is a kill shelter." At the time, I was living in USFS barracks, and could not take him there. But the thought of a kill shelter was impossible. He was just a little puppy.

I phoned my boyfriend and asked if we could take in another dog. We had a four-year-old pit bull mix rescue named Patty, and through persuasion, he agreed we could take him. Excited, I called the kill shelter and made arrangements to pick up Seamus as soon as I could get off work. On a prolonged four-day weekend, I ventured down to Visalia to pick him up. When I took him in my arms, I felt relieved, and knew he would be safe and have a great home with our family. Seamus and I had a long drive ahead from the valley to where we lived on Lake Tahoe—a total drive of about six hours. The drive was quiet as he sat in his little box, staring up at me with his big brown eyes.

Seamus is now four years old, and is an awesome dog. At first, he was afraid of snow, due to his experience, but now loves it as well as water, which he can never resist waddling in. He is afraid to be left alone, and follows us closely wherever we go. As a pit bull, he is a sensitive boy, afraid of cats, but a lover of other dogs. I am so glad he is a part of my life.

MAYA

THANKS TO CANDICE MUGGLIN

I would like to share the story of my beloved rescue pit bull that was known at the shelter as "Mama" but I lovingly refer to as "Maya."

According to the rescue I got her from, she was nothing more than a baby factory, and was found roaming the streets. My angel was saved from a high kill shelter by a wonderful person with a soft heart for Maya. She was sentenced to death simply because of her breed, and her dislike of other dogs. The person at the shelter arranged for a transfer for Maya because she was just too sweet and friendly to be sentenced to such an unnecessary death.

Maya sat at yet another shelter, unwanted.

The people at the shelter loved her and spoiled her rotten, trying to make her life less lonely. Thankfully, one of the volunteers there knew my mom and told her about this wonderful dog, after finding out I was looking for a new member of my family. I went to visit this sweet girl and fell in love instantly. She is my life, and the best thing that has ever happened to me. She is not perfect, but has a heart of gold. She can be unpredictable around other dogs, but even that can be managed. I love my dog, and could not care less that she is a pit bull. To me, she is Maya, and it does not matter to me what her breed is, it does not change how much I love her.

ROSIE

THANKS TO CATHY CLARK

This story is about a brindle and white female pit bull now named Rosie. She was dumped on a country road here in East Texas back in late May, 2012.

I first heard about her from a post on Facebook. A woman posted that someone had dumped a pregnant pit bull down the road from her house. The dog had been there for a few days and this woman had been taking her food. The woman was getting really concerned for her, because the dog was pregnant and looked like she was getting close to whelping. The dog stayed right at that spot and did not wander too far from where she had been abandoned.

I shared the post and the dog's plight with my husband. We were hesitant to rescue this girl, not knowing how she was raised. I retired from a local municipality and worked twenty-five years as the director of Animal Control and Shelter. I had more incidents than I can or want to count that dealt with people that fought their dogs. I did not want to put my other dogs, my husband, or myself in danger of being bitten or attacked. Our area was a popular area for dog fighting.

I woke up several times during the night wondering and worrying about this dog. I knew if she was aggressive I just could not help her, but there is always that "what if." I got up at 5:00 the next morning and sat down at the computer to see what the weather was going to be, and saw that rain was headed our way. Radar showed a severe thunderstorm with possible winds up to 60 mph, and heavy rain. My thoughts immediately went to the pregnant pit bull! So

I gave in, and left the hubby a note; I was headed to rescue the pregnant pit bull.

It was already getting dark and stormy looking outside. I drove right to the location and there she was lying curled up on the embankment of the ditch. She stood up and looked at me with the most pleading eyes. I rolled down the window and asked her, "Hey girl, what did you do to deserve this?" She hung her head and started walking toward my car. When she got to the edge of the road I opened my door and talked to her some more to see how she would react before I got out and approached her.

She lied down and rolled over on her back and rolled down into the ditch. She was so fat from being pregnant she could not maneuver to get herself back up because of the incline of the ditch on both sides of her. So I went down and helped her roll over. She wagged her tail and kept her head low, like she was being scolded. I tried coaxing her around to the passenger side where I had a sheet over the seat, but she was leery of following, so I opened the door, picked her up and put her in the car. She looked up at me with those big golden eyes, and tears poured out of my eyes for this poor girl.

As I turned around to head home, I asked, "What happened to you sweetie? Were you a thorn in someone's side and they dumped you with no regrets?" I told her that her name would be Rosie—she may have been a thorn in someone else's side, but she would be my Rose.

She had eight beautiful pit bull puppies a week later. I had lain by her kennel when the first was born stayed until she had the last. When the puppies were weaned they were taken to an animal shelter that is pit bull friendly. There, the adoption process could begin and the puppies could go to loving families. Rose has turned out to be a very special girl; she is smart, loving and gets along with all my other dogs. Because of my wonderful Rosie, we have rescued two other female pit bulls. We love our pitties—most of all, my wonderful Rose.

MORGAN

THANKS TO DEBBIE McADAMS

My brother had the last living offspring of Petey from "Our Gang," who just recently died at nearly eighteen years old. He has had pits for over thirty years, so I, too, grew to love them. Eight and a half years ago we adopted a pit mix named Morgan who was only eleven and a half pounds at three months old. She and her three siblings were brought to a no-kill shelter (Animal Orphanage) in Voorhees, New Jersey. They all had Parvo. Sadly, two of them died, but the other two were fosters until they were well enough to go to the shelter.

Morgan was on two different antibiotics, as she was still recovering from Parvo and had an upper respiratory infection. She was skin and bones, too sickly to even undergo spaying, as required before animals can leave the shelter.

I begged and pleaded with them to let me adopt her or she was going to die. They did. She is a healthy, vibrant, amazingly loyal member of our family. She loves everyone and sings—I have video! I will always own a pit and champion their cause to promote breed awareness.

PHOENIX

THANKS TO KIMBERLY BANKS

I rescued my pit bull from a parking lot at six months old. She was half-starved and in desperate need of help. Now, she is the funniest dog I have ever seen. Due to the choke chain that I removed, she cannot bark, so she yodels. The vet said she does not know if Phoenix will ever bark but it is not painful to her. It just adds to her goofy charm!

My first funny story we remember is Phoenix being a "land shark." My husband and I were lying on the bed, with our feet dangling and I noticed Phoenix doing an army crawl from the doorway of the bedroom. I pointed her out and my husband and I laughed as she realized she had been spotted. She laid her head down trying to act naturally. We continued our conversation and she started creeping toward us again. We were only half paying attention to the big goofball as she inched closer and closer. All of a sudden my husband yelped in surprise and Phoenix was wearing a smugly satisfied look on her face. My husband started to laugh. Our "land shark" snuck up on him and nibbled his toe. She always keeps us on our toes. She is such a goofy puppy!

Another story is "Phoenix the Spider Slayer." I am afraid of spiders, so when I called my son to kill one, he worked for ten minutes to get it caught and released outside. Phoenix went out with him. My son turned the spider loose safely outside and Phoenix pounced on it. I heard my son crying, "Noooooooo!" I looked outside to see Phoenix crunching on the spider. My son was upset for all of 10 seconds until Phoenix gave him that goofy yodel—then the spider was forgotten and he was laughing at her. She still rescues me from those creepy eight-legged critters. There is never a dull moment with Phoenix!

LINDA

THANKS TO KELLY TURNBULL

This is a story about Linda, a dog who was unfortunate enough to be born in Ontario, barely a year before breed specific legislation was introduced in the province. From what I understand, she was mistreated in her puppyhood and used as breeding stock. She was seized by animal control just after the ban was placed. The nine puppies she was pregnant with were immediately taken from her after she gave birth, and were killed. I do not use the word euthanize in this context as there was nothing merciful about their death. She was passed from shelter to shelter all over Ontario and ended up in Toronto, where I live.

It was the year of my thirtieth birthday and I was still fairly new to the city. I had come to Toronto to go to school and had recently finished my studies. I had just ended a five-year relationship, of which two were long distance, and decided to stay. I knew I had always wanted a dog of my own and was considering it within the next few years, but unsure I was ready for that. I had no problem with pit bulls as a breed but was looking more in the direction of a bulldog of some sort.

Then I heard about the ban.

I knew what would happen to all these dogs in the shelters, and while any "pit bull type" dog born before the ban was grandfathered in and allowed to live, the chances of them being adopted with all the demonization of them flying around was slim to none.

So, I decided to adopt a pit bull for my birthday. I looked online at the shelters but at that time, few pit bulls were being offered for adoption. Shelter staff and management were confused (or did not care) about the grandfathered clause and were killing them as they came in.

I found Linda on the Toronto Animal Control website and was smitten immediately. On the morning of my birthday I asked my friends to take me down to the shelter so I could meet her. While we were waiting in the lobby, a staff member walked by and the dog she was walking came directly over to me. It was Linda.

I spent some time with her in the visitation room while my friends patiently waited outside. After 20 minutes I walked out and asked where I could fill out the adoption application. It was clear the staff there loved her and wanted her to find a home, because five minutes after completing the form, they said I could take her right then and there. Not prepared for the quick turnaround time, as I thought the process would take longer, I asked if I could pick her up the next day. They normally are not open on Sundays but one of the staff said she would come in first thing specifically, so I could prepare. I spent the rest of my birthday in pet stores, calling everyone with the news and puppy proofing my apartment.

As a first time dog owner on my own, I was ecstatic. I read every book I could get my hands on, turning down almost every party I was invited to, and spent every moment I could with her. Everything was great...for a while.

About two months in, we started having issues. She was clearly fearful of men and as her comfort with me in her new home environment grew, behavioral issues came to the fore. She began barking at men on the street and none of my male friends could come into my house. I knew we had a problem.

I immediately searched online and canvassed pet stores looking for a trainer to help me. More than once, they would tell me that there was nothing that could be done to resolve the situation. "Pit bulls are just like that," I was told. I spent weeks crying myself to sleep, desperate to find a solution.

I began obsessively reading more intensive training and animal behavior books, every article I could find and asking everyone who had a dog for advice. With what I was learning and applying, she gradually began to improve.

I joined sprouting "pit bull" groups to meet with like-minded people and attempt to socialize her, though the required muzzles and short leashes made it difficult. I became politically involved. I went to endless protests to overturn the ban and spent every spare moment going to meetings, writing letters to politicians and educating people about the ban at dog shows and events.

Then one day it hit me like a ton of bricks. I walked out of my day job one Friday and never looked back. I was going to help animals. It was my calling and my passion.

I worked at vets offices, as a dog walker and at a no kill shelter. I became a dog trainer.

Linda has saved my life in more ways than I can count. She has changed me for the better, gave me the courage to follow my dreams and taught me how to be a better person.

She chose me, and she saved me, and it is all because she is a pit bull.

JAIDA AND TANK

THANKS TO ELIZABETH KOEGLER

In December 2009, I received a phone call that a litter of pit bull puppies needed help. Our neighbor was the dog warden of Guilford, Connecticut. She heard of a situation that did not seem right, so we drove about twenty-five miles to Southington, Connecticut. We pulled up to the house and at first glance, thought it condemned but it was not. The residents were backyard breeders who bred an eleven-month-old pit bull puppy, trying to make some easy money. When the dog rejected the little ones, they proceeded to drown the puppies. We arrived to find three puppies still alive. They were only two weeks old. We took all of them with us.

Sadly, the female did not make it, but the two males survived. I got up every two hours to boil water, let it cool, mix the formula and feed them. They slept on my chest in blankets for weeks because they were so small. The vet told me the chances of them making it were very slim, so I got up every two hours to check on them, praying they would still be alive.

Now, almost four years later, they are healthy big boys. The black pit bull's name is Jaida. He is almost seventy pounds and is an amazing dog. His brother Tank, who lives with my mother, is fifty pounds and thriving with his brother and sister. They are a very strong breed with a lot of heart and soul. I hope this story touches your heart like these pups have stolen mine!

FAUSTO

THANKS TO ADRIEN ZAP

I have been an animal lover all of my life and for as long as I can remember, I wanted to be a veterinarian. When it came time to apply to schools, I discovered that there are few accredited veterinary schools in the United States and, unless you are a resident of the state where the school is located, your chances of being accepted into one of these programs is slim to none.

Not about to give up on my dream, I began applying to schools in the Caribbean and was accepted at St. George's University (SGU) in Grenada. SGU earned U.S. accreditation in 2011 and is only the second Caribbean institution to be accredited. Students in this program are nearly all Americans. We spend three years studying in Grenada and a fourth year at a veterinary teaching hospital in the United States.

Moving to Grenada was quite a culture shock, having come from a suburban town in southwestern Connecticut. In Grenada, animals are typically seen roaming the streets, so much so that it is difficult to know which ones belong to someone and which are strays. Most of the dogs seen loose are mixed breed dogs the locals call "pot hounds," likely because they drink out of pot holes in the streets.

Pets are normally left outside and their care consists of putting down food and water. Many have untreated fleas, ticks, etc. Unlike American culture, this is not considered neglect in Grenada. The treatment of pets is just different. Unfortunately though, permeating through Caribbean society the same as in American culture, are the myths and stereotypes surrounding certain breeds of dogs. In neighboring Trinidad and Tobago there is a Dangerous Dog Act in effect, making it illegal to own a pit bull, a Fila Brasileiro, a Japanese Tosa or any similar dog, or any individual dog that the local government deems dangerous, without a government authorized permit. In Grenada, pit bulls are universally feared and not allowed loose like other dogs. Those who do get out are often brought in to us with machete wounds. This is not because these people want to hurt the dogs, but because they are afraid and feel the need to defend themselves, even if the dogs have shown no aggression at all.

In January, 2013, I was sent with another student to the Grenada SPCA. I was greeted by many dogs of all ages, shapes and sizes running around the yard. Since there are so many, any visitors to the shelter are seen as potential adopters and I was no exception. Even though I had no intention of adopting a dog that day, a shelter employee urged me to meet a little three-legged pit bull puppy who was a new arrival.

Fausto adopted me that day. He was just shy of three months old and had just lost his left hind leg. His owner had brought him in with his paw entangled in a wire. When the owner learned that the infection had spread and he would lose his leg, the owner decided he no longer wanted the puppy and left him at the shelter.

I now know why they call it love at first sight. He looked at me with his big hazel (slightly crossed) eyes and I was hooked. Fausto is now fourteen months old and the biggest source of joy in my life! Playing with him is the perfect stress reliever after a long day of classes. He has accompanied me back and forth between Grenada and my home in Connecticut. Everywhere we go, people always stop and ask about him, probably because he is missing a leg and also because they realize he is a pit bull. He does just about everything a normal dog does. He can run, jump and even swim!

As in the United States, pit bulls are held to a higher standard in Grenada. Everything they do is highly scrutinized and their behavior must be impeccable at all times. Fausto has not only stepped up, he has embraced the role. We take every chance we get to talk to people and to educate them. Fausto is the love of my life and an ambassador for his breed.

HUDSON

THANKS TO RICHARD NASH

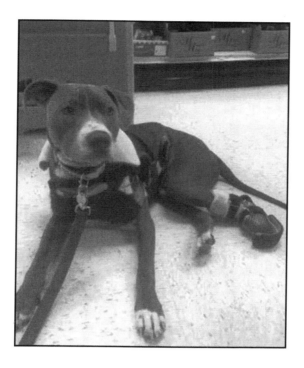

My name is Hudson. I am a Blue Nose Pit Bull and this is my story.

On Saturday, September 8, 2012, railroad workers found me and my two sisters nailed by our paws to the railroad tracks in Albany, New York. We were only three weeks old. We were taken to Mohawk Hudson Humane Society (MHHS) in Menands, New York, where we were given life-saving treatment for dehydration, malnutrition, infection and the injuries to our paws. My parents and some of my other siblings were also found nearby in the back of a U-Haul truck. Fortunately they were rescued too, but sadly one of my sisters did not make it.

On September 13, 2012, veterinary surgeon Dr. Tom Bowersox was called in to assess our condition. Dr. Bowersox determined that because I was still so young, rather than amputate my entire leg, he would try fitting me with a prosthetic limb. My sister Pearl lost two of her toes, but was going to be okay.

On October 12, 2012, Dr. Bowersox fitted my first prosthetic paw and a month later it was put in place. I would need several prosthetic paws as I grew up, but for now, we were ready to find our forever homes.

On November 9, 2012, MHHS announced that any interested forever families should write essays of no more than 300 words as to why they wanted to adopt me and my sister Pearl. Then on November 30, 2012, I met my future family, Rich, Rosemarie and Sami Nash. My family lives near the shelter. My mom Rosemarie works from home and my dad Rich is self-employed and has the time to take me to my appointments and for training classes.

Before they could adopt me, though, I had to meet my sister Sami. Sami is a pit bull mix. She was found as a stray and had been staying at our doctor's office for almost ten weeks when our dad Rich happened to stop by the office. Our mom and dad decided to adopt her and took her home. Sami and I first met at the shelter and hit it off immediately. It was like we had been best friends forever. Even now she always looks out for me like the awesome big sister that she is.

It was announced on December 5, 2012, that I would have a forever home with the Nash family, and my sister Pearl, would be going to another loving home. Now, Pearl and I have play dates at least once a month and more often when the weather is nice.

Not long after I went home, I started my training. First I took a basic obedience class and then a good manners class. Then I received my Canine Good Citizen badge and most recently I received my Therapy Dog International Therapy Dog Certification.

My dad and I have visited sick children at St. Catherine's Center and we attend many fundraising events. My dad likes to say I have more of a social life than he does! Eventually we want to visit wounded warriors at Veterans hospitals. I hope I can make them feel better, show them lots of love and help them to overcome obstacles just like I did.

I now live with not only my parents and sister Sami but also five indoor cats. Some other cats have also adopted our family. Apparently no one wanted them so they came to our house. They live outside but come into our garage and basement when it is cold out or when they are hungry. Sami, the cats and I all snuggle together, clean each other and give each other kisses. My dad likes to say that if we all do right by each other then we can all live together in harmony. Dad thinks this is a good lesson for everyone and so do we.

I still have nightmares sometimes and I also have some challenges to overcome. I have allergies, but my parents take very good care of me and buy me special food to keep me healthy. I am still getting used to my new paw. I can run but jumping is another story, so my parents have to lift me into the car and up onto the bed. I have trouble with the stairs sometimes, but I am getting better. I know that I have the best home any dog could ask for and I am grateful for my family every day. I am determined to face these challenges and prove that I can be like any other dog. I also hope to share this optimism to help humans who are dealing with their own struggles.

Every once in a while when I am out with my family, we meet people that do not like me and Sami just because of our breed. We just cannot understand it because we are always nice to everyone we meet. I guess some people just will not know or care enough to learn about us, but my family and I keep trying to educate and lead by example.

I am actually famous now. I have my own Facebook page and fans in over twenty countries. Some people write to me and tell me that they never liked pit bulls but they have changed their minds after reading about me. So many people have said nice things about me. People have even said they were going to visit shelters in their areas so they could meet other pit bulls and maybe even volunteer to take them out for walks, and all because of me! It makes me happy when I can help other dogs.

Even though a person once hurt me, I am not angry. I can look at people and just love them. The best thing is that my dad decided, because of me and Sami, that he wants to become a dog trainer and he is going to school for it now. One of the trainers he works with has a sister who owns one of the Vicktory dogs (for those of you who do not know, these are the dogs that were rescued from the fighting ring run by football player Michael Vick). I will never understand why some people want to hurt us.

Dad says he found his calling. I am not sure what that means but he sure seems happy these days. He not only hopes to train dogs, but he also hopes to educate people about pit bulls. He hopes to change stereotypes and change people's minds when it comes to dogs like me and Sami. He always says, "It's not about me, it's about the dogs."

From all of us in the Nash family, we hope you have a woof-tastic day! https://www.facebook.com/HudsonTheRailroadPuppy

LUCIA AND TYE

THANKS TO ERICA KUTZING

Lucia

Tye

When I saw Lucia's face in her intake photo, there was immediate connection. I am a volunteer for Save-A-Pet Animal Rescue and Guardians of Rescue.

I had no idea of how intense the process would be for getting this dog, and the subsequent care she would need. Thanks to *many* volunteers who stayed up late to help me learn some of the ropes and get into contact with the right people, Lucia's life was spared. These are people I have never met before that came together and worked tirelessly to save a dog none of us had met. Those people alone restored my faith in the human race.

Save-A-Pet Animal Rescue, an organization that I have been a part of for fourteen years, pulled her for me and arranged transport.

Lucia had only hours to live as she was at the end of her hold. What made it worse was she had a large cancerous tumor on her face. It was about the size of an orange and was protruding from her mouth. I threw all caution to the wind and welcomed her into my home.

I brought her to so many vets, opting to go with holistic medication rather than surgery. Lucia also had a cancerous mass in her chest. Surgery was out of the question. I kept her comfortable for 3 months. That was 3 months of trips to the beach, delicious steaks, cuddles in the grass, and even a party for her where all of her fans could meet her (she had a Facebook page with over 7,500 followers).

My Lucia passed away September 29th, exactly three months after her initial euthanasia date. I was absolutely heartbroken but I knew our time would be short. I gave her what her other family could not-peace before she went to the bridge.

I have a special place in my heart for special needs animals. My pit bull Tye (2 years old) was born blind. I fostered him at 2 weeks old and fell in love. We have been together ever since. I also have 2 one-eyed cats and many other furry kids. https://www.facebook. com/lucialongisland?ref=br_tf

PUMA

THANKS TO JACQUELINE DRAKE

I am a 22 years old and in college working towards a degree in veterinary medicine. I am also an intern with a pit bull rescue and rehabilitation facility called Detroit Bully Corps. I got involved with volunteering at rescues a year ago and figured out quickly that my passion is with the "bullies." I was about four years old when my parents brought home their first rescue pit bull straight out of a fighting ring—he was a mess. After some love and care from them he became my best friend who played with Barbie dolls and dressed up with me. I guess you could say I was ruined right from the start.

Fast forward to March of 2013. I landed an internship/volunteer position with Villalobos Rescue Center in New Orleans, Louisiana. It was a weeklong position and one of the responsibilities we were given was to really work (socialize, play, walk, spend one-on-one time) with Tia's "special" group of pitties. There were about fourteen altogether. These were the dogs that could not handle kennel life, as it was too stressful or overwhelming. One of the fourteen was my newly adopted senior girl, Puma. She spent her whole life, more than nine years, in rescue facilities, starting at eight months old. She suffers from PTSD from an event that happened when she was very young. Her condition used to completely rule her mentally and physically. Loud noises (a bag dropping, thunder, someone yelling) would actually make her pass out, until I came along.

She was officially adopted in May. She is ten years old and acts like she is two, (especially when presented with a tennis ball). She came into a home with four cats, and four humans (me included) and she loves us all like she has lived with us forever.

Puma breaks out of her shell more and more every day. She loves attention and is very demanding. If my mom is cooking she will just come lean on her for some back scratches or sit and give eye contact until she is given tons of treats—because, well, she deserves all of them! She does the best wiggle-dance for anyone that comes home or even for guests. She is extremely respectful and well trained. She has met other furry members of the family, including her cousin Ranger the Golden Retriever and Riley the Jack Russell. She is more than happy to take long strolls down the trails with them and is your average bully—resilient, and always smiling.

We all call her our family therapy dog because she is always there when we each individually need her.

Puma and I were featured on an episode of *Pit Bulls and Parolees* this year, so please be sure and look for us!

MAMA JADE

THANKS TO CHRISTIANNA WILLIS

"Your Pit Bull found me and I am not giving her back" – The Craig's List Post that went viral…..

"Last Friday night, your dog wandered up onto our porch. Signs of the abuse she had somehow escaped, riddled her body. The fresh bite marks on her muzzle, the scars that covered her body, the exposed pink and purple flesh around her neck, where she was obviously tied up with ropes that cut their way into her skin, over and over again. There were obvious signs that she had been bred relentlessly - time after time. The pressure wounds on her elbows that bled whenever they touched anything, from being tied and forced to lay on cement ground and metal cage mesh.

None of those things are even the worst part. Upon examining her teeth to gauge her approximate age, I burst into tears. I found that you had pulled the majority of them out and the ones that were left were had been filed down. And you did this without anesthesia, this I am sure of. You did this so she could not fight back. You did this so she could not injure any dogs you had trained to fight-when you threw her in there with them. With each bite of her they took and each yelp she cried, they would look at you for reassurance. Because all they wanted to do was please you. Loyalty is in their blood. Violence is not.

The first night she was here, I stayed up with her and only slept for 2 hours. Every time I would move, she would get up and look at me with worry-stricken eyes. She did not want me to leave her.

Somehow, God must have led this mama to my doorstep, knowing she would find comfort here. The next morning, I took her to my work on my day off, as I work at an animal hospital.

Upon entering the building, her neck started to bleed. The thick collar which you put on her caused tender scars on her neck. She never even yelped. I discovered it as I was weighing her and saw blood on the scale. I took the ridiculous thing off of her.

The amazing people I work with have all fallen head over heels in love with your dog. So when we discovered she had breast cancer, it broke our hearts even more.

Over the last three days, our staff has grown to love this beautiful and broken soul. Skin and bones, we feed her constantly but only foods that are soft enough for her. You know, since you ripped her teeth out and all.

Mama lets you get right up in her face. In fact, she LOVES it. She will give you slobbery kisses and nuzzle your face with love.

We are all amazed at how trusting of humans she is. Dogs however, completely terrify her. It does not matter the size, she growls in fear and tucks her tail between her legs. But who can blame her? After what you did to her?

Tomorrow, Mama will finally feel peace. And when she closes her eyes and takes her last breath, I will be there. I will hold her big old head and I will tell her how much I love her.

And when her soul has left her battered body and I have dried the tears enough to see, I will document every bruise, every bite, every cut, scrape and gash. I will photograph her teeth, or rather, where her teeth used to be. I will turn in all the evidence and post it where EVERYONE will see it. I will use it to educate kids in heavily crime ridden areas, on the horrors of dog fighting.

If you could do that to a dog, you should not be allowed in everyday society. Teaching our children right from wrong is the only way to put a stop to this.

One day, you will be caught. If I ever find out who did this to the dog we all lovingly knew as "Mama Jade" I honestly do not know what I would do. But it would probably involve contacting your mother and informing her of what a monster she managed to raise. My goal would be to make a mockery out of your pathetic life.

Mama Jade's story will not be silenced. She just happened to show up on the doorstep of one extremely persistent, intelligent, respected and now angry human being."

The story does not end here, though!

Upon learning that she had cancer, we had initially decided it would be best to humanely euthanize her because she had already experienced so much pain in her life. I signed the papers but decided last minute that I would put it off until the next day. That night, I became outraged at the thought of how horrible her life had been. I posted the ad on Craigslist as a way to vent my frustrations. Never once did I think it would reach so many people.

After realizing just how many people were behind her, it became apparent that this girl was not quite ready to leave us just yet. I created a "Mama Jade's Cancer Treatment Fund." Thanks to the outpouring of support from so many caring people, Mama Jade received the treatment she needed and is now cancer free. She will finally have the chance to live a beautiful life and know love as every dog should.

Dog fighting is a terrible and cruel "sport" that is often times swept under the rug. Animal abuse is often times punished with a slap on the wrist and the cycle just continues.

Many have e-mailed me with incredible words of support, calling me an "angel" or a "hero" and although it warms my heart-at the same time it makes me sad. I was just doing what any person with a pulse would (or apparently should) do if they encountered an animal that desperately needed help.

The world would be a much better place if people could just take a moment out of their busy lives-to help a creature that would do anything for you in return. https://www.facebook.com/MamaJadeNashville

PART THREE

BEST FRIENDS

"The most I can do for my friend is simply to be his friend. I have no wealth to bestow on him. If he knows that I am happy in loving him, he will want no other reward. Is not friendship divine in this?"

~ Henry David Thoreau

PIPER AND BABE

THANKS TO JULIE FREE

We were not looking for a pit bull. When we met Piper, the girl in the center, she was a scrawny pup at Chouteau Pound Pals, a shelter in a small town east of Tulsa. We just thought she was a typical mix of some kind. One day our vet called her a "nice little pit mix." We knew nothing about pits other than what you hear on the news. We had our aging dogs, one a Beagle, the other a Jack Russell, so we were worried. After doing some research, we took her to a dog school, took some classes, and even started doing some agility with her (for the record she is terrified of the Beagle and the Jack Russell). We could not ask for a sweeter dog.

Enter the three-legged goat, GP (Goat Puppy). When he was born, I thought he was dead, my husband was at work and I was playing goat midwife. GP was one of triplets. I brought his still body inside to put on a heating pad. Piper had started licking her, gradually bringing him around to where he was at least responsive. GP's mother wanted nothing to do with him or his siblings, so they hung out with Piper. They played in the yard while she supervised their bottle feeding, etc. GP's siblings went to live with our neighbors as pets and we let Piper keep GP. GP broke his back leg and wound up having part of it amputated.

Piper has become the spokes-dog for our local pound. She and GP appear at rescue events and prior to his injury, he followed her over agility obstacles. During all of this, I started volunteering to help the pound with basic obedience training for the adoptable dogs.

Babe, (the white pit), was a longtime resident of the pound. The information on her cage said she had to be an only dog. She learned some basic commands pretty quickly, but we could not find the right home for her. In Dec of 2012, she hurt her back foot. She had gotten it hung up in the wire around her kennel at the pound, (she had been there since November 2011). Eventually she had to have three toes amputated and needed a foster home while she recovered. We brought her home and kept her away from the other dogs at first. Gradually, we started introducing her to the other dogs and she was wonderful with them. She even got along with Piper's goat!

We declared Babe a foster failure a few months ago. Now I bring Babe to the pound along with Piper to test the pound dogs' behavior around other dogs. She is amazing (another lap dog that is scared of the Beagle and Jack Russell). Her foot barely slows her down and we found out she can compete in UKC (United Kennel

Club) agility. She has completed one agility class and will be in her first competition in March of 2014. The foot injury was awful, but it turned out to be a blessing in disguise. Otherwise, we would have never known what an awesome dog she turned out to be.

CEASAR, MR BOLT AND HOPE

THANKS TO MARY AND SCOTT LAMBERT

One day my husband and I dropped off our chocolate Lab for grooming and on our way out of the facility, there was a rescue called Benji's Buddies. We saw some adorable puppies and had to stop. Apollo or Ceasar–we could not decide. Ceasar came and gave me some amazing kisses. Apollo was mellow, yet huge and adorable. I told my husband I wanted the kisser! We had no idea what breed he was and Toni, rescue goddess, said their mother was there, too, and there she was–a huge pit bull! My husband and I never sought after a pit and did not want to appear ignorant, but Toni could see we were taken aback by her size and look. She also had the father. All had been abandoned. The dad was an American Bulldog and brindle like Ceasar. We told her we would like to adopt the brindle puppy named Ceasar.

My husband and I were going through empty nest syndrome and feeling rather lonely. We took Ceasar home and never imagined this sweet four month old puppy would literally save our hearts. We both had dogs all our lives, but never a pit bull. I bought books so we would know what we were getting into, and we socialized him at the dog park and took him for daily walks. Oh, we had challenges! He ate my favorite couch, foot stools, all four corners of the coffee table, but he never was anything but an oversized lap dog that wanted our love. We lived through the challenges and fell in love with the breed!

When we lost our third dog, Ginger (a Chow Chow), I was devastated. She had been with us since she was a puppy. She went to Rainbow Bridge at age 14. My husband said that in her honor, we needed to rescue another pit bull. We went back to Toni, who was now with Little Rascals Rescue. She brought us a beautiful white female. She was one year old and had just lost her liter of eight. Her old owner had left her howling in pain and a neighbor took her from their yard to the vet. Her puppies had passed and were still inside her, which almost killed her. They saved this beautiful baby and we had to have her. We named her Hope, in hope she would never feel pain again. It took her several months to trust my husband, obviously a fear of men, but now she gives kisses whenever she can, and we catch her doing a happy dance every morning, as if to say, "I love my family!"

Then Toni emailed us and showed us a picture of another white pit. He got a skin disease in the shelter that ate his skin on his chest. They had to cut it out and wait for it to grow back. He was rather homely, but we said we would meet him. My husband and I said, "We are just meeting him, we have three dogs already." Well, you know how this ends. We now have Mr. Bolt too, who grew out of his homeliness and is now quite handsome. I am in love with my Lab, but have never felt the warmth and devotion I have felt with our three rescued pits. They are our world and we both work daily to share our story with friends and strangers. We are on our fourth couch but we would not change a thing. This breed healed our lonely hearts, and when our beautiful ten-year-old Lab has to leave us for doggy heaven, we know already that we will rescue yet another in her honor. Here is a picture of our babies, in order - Ceasar, Mr. Bolt, Bobbi the Lab and Hope. Who rescued who?

This breed changed our lives, and definitely for the better. Plus the commission the furniture stores are getting makes them love them too. Best breed ever!

DEMON

THANKS TO AMELIA RODRIGUEZ

A friend of mine had a pit bull puppy named Demon. He was a little black ball of fur and love. She had to move and when she did she left him with her son, my boyfriend and me. Eventually my boyfriend and I moved out and Demon stayed with her son. We moved next door and saw them fairly regularly. However, being new parents to a less than a 12-month-old child, we had not noticed when we saw him less and less.

One day my boyfriend came home and told me our friend was getting rid of Demon. We could not understand why, he was such a good dog. We went and knocked on the door and he said, "I just do not want to take care of him anymore, he is gross and annoying." We walked into the kitchen and the smell was immediate. There is really no way to describe it other than putrid. We heard his tail banging against the inside of the plastic crate in the center of the kitchen floor. We looked in the crate and found the saddest looking creature we had ever seen.

He was sitting in his own feces with a filthy bowl of what I assume was once water next to the wire kennel door. There were tiny flies everywhere and he was incessantly scratching and whining while he wagged his tail and tried to lick us through the wire. We opened the kennel to let him out and we both gasped. He wiggled excitedly as he stepped out into the light and whimpered as he moved because across his back, his tail, his chest, face and legs were stripes of red and green. His fleas practically galloped through the festering open sores all across his body and he cried out when he tried to scratch his neck because he was quite literally ripping himself apart trying to find some relief.

I cried on the spot. I dropped to my knees and sobbed and hugged this poor creature. He just licked me and wagged his nearly furless tail. I told his owner to gather up whatever he had for him and give it to me. In return we would only call his mother and not the police.

We brought him to the vet who literally had to shave him to see the full extent of the damage. He was shaved, bathed, dressed, coned and given antibiotics. When offered food or water, he basically never chewed, but immediately swallowed, inhaling every meal or drink was if it were his last.

We brought him home, hesitant at first, though, to let him near our son. He had been around our son before and was always wonderful but we knew he had been through a lot. We soon discovered that we had nothing to worry about. Every time my little boy cried, there was the nanny dog pushing his way through anything in his path. He would go sniff my son and kiss him to make him feel better. When my son crawled around, Demon followed him, ears perked, ready for adventure. Eventually they became "team destruction". My son would roll his walker into the gate and knock it down so Demon could get into the kitchen. Then he would follow his four-legged brother and pull down the garbage can so Demon could feast, and he could laugh at his silly friend's butt sticking out of the can.

Today my son and Demon are both three years old. They are still the best of friends. They do everything from eating, to napping, to watching Spongebob together. Demon is not only my son's best friend, he is also the one who keeps me together. I suffer from severe anxiety and manic depression. My boyfriend left and I lost everything. All I took from my apartment to my mother's house were a few bags of clothes, some of my son's toys, a few pictures and my beloved dog. I remember my mom being so worried about having a pit bull move into her house. "When he has finished running around like a lunatic, what does he do?" she asked me." "He lies down and loves you," was the best answer I could give her. He changed her mind about pit bulls within the first week of being there.

At that point in my life I cried daily. I could barely eat or sleep. The only reasons I had to get up in the morning were my boys. Every night Demon would lie on the couch with me and lick away my tears until I fell asleep. He is to this day, the biggest cuddle bug I have ever met. He is sixty-five pounds of lap dog. After everything he has been through, it still astounds me that he could ever forgive people the way he has. Anyone who comes to my house is shocked by my sweet pibble and the fact that he just cannot stop kissing them.

Our lives have changed a lot together. We moved from my mother's, and I am now engaged. Demon has an adopted sister, Jennifer the bulldog, whose owner is currently serving in Afghanistan. My fiancée knows when I have an anxiety attack or just feeling blue, my dog is the only one who can drag me out of it. Demon is the most loving creature I have ever come across on this earth, and I thank God for him all the time.

MAJOR

THANKS TO ANNA MATARESE

I have so many stories that I could tell about my baby Major, but one in particular, is when we brought him to the dog park with a friend who had just gotten a Dachshund. All the other dogs started growling and trying to bite the Dachshund. Their owners did nothing, but Major, my pit bull, ran to his little friend and not once did he growl or bark but hovered over the Dachshund to protect him. Our whole neighborhood loves Major and he is now a big brother to our baby girl.

MISS PIGGY

THANKS TO ANNE DOBNAK

I adopted an American Staffordshire in June, 2013. Her name is Miss Piggy and she has been an absolute life saver and life changer.

Growing up, my mom refused to allow me to own a pit bull, so naturally, the first thing I did when I got an apartment of my own was go to the local shelter and pick one out. At first, my heart was set on another pit bull named Sage, but unfortunately, she was too cat-aggressive. My roommate has a cat named Effy. As you can imagine, I was devastated. Around this same time one of the volunteers begged me to meet Minnie, who was running out of time. No one had shown any interest in her.

I reluctantly agreed. Once she was out, I was absolutely in love. I knew she was going to come home with me, and she did, receiving the new name of Miss Piggy.

When we first found each other, she was overweight. This was from being bred so much and she was still lactating. The shelter did not receive any puppies with her, so the worst is assumed for her last litter. However, her life changed for the best.

Miss Piggy snorts when she is happy. She is my emotional support animal and keeps me going on the days I am so depressed that I just want to lay in bed. She supports me and lies down with me. She licks my face to tell me when it is time for her walk and breakfast. We will often lay in bed together until noon before it is time for her walk. She understands me more than any other dog that has ever been in my life.

My so-called vicious pit bull plays with my roommate's cat, jumping all over the place with him and sharing toys. She attacks my eleven year old nephew with kisses and tail wags. Miss Piggy has changed not only my mother's mind, but the rest of the family's mind on squashing the myths that pits are vicious dogs. My mom is often more than willing to watch Miss Piggy for the day as she just blends in with my mom's five cats, Boston Terrier Winston and the Rat Terrier, Spencer. We call her a giant cat. I have never met a more loving personality, except in other pit bulls.

Back in September, 2013, Miss Piggy had what we believed to be a tumor on her leg. Devastated, I was willing to pay anything to keep her alive. Thankfully it was only an infection, but it has caused her to have leg problems that she will most likely deal with for life. She cannot jump up on the couches or beds anymore without falling, but that never keeps her down. She just props herself halfway up and looks to you to help her finish the job, smiling and wagging her tail the entire time. Once she is up, she immediately crawls into your lap and looks at you, questioning why her ears are not being rubbed by you yet.

Miss Piggy is my own personal angel, and every day I thank fate for bringing us together the way that it did. She has changed not only my life, but the minds of many others and continues to change minds every day with her Facebook page. Using her page, we help find homes for other homeless animals and advocate for the breed, demanding the end of Breed Specific Legislation (BSL).

I recently received a message on her page from a mother telling me how she reads Miss Piggy's posts out loud to her four year old son and how he squeals in delight and loves to follow her. I told him that Miss Piggy loved him very much and he blushed and said,

"She loves me?!" I almost cannot believe the impact Miss Piggy has had on my life in such a short time, but I am not at all surprised at the loving personality of a pit bull. https://www.facebook.com/ MissPiggyThePitty

LUCKY

THANKS TO LAURA CLARK

I have a beautiful pit bull named Lucky.

We discovered him in a shopping cart with two sisters at five weeks old.

He was left there by someone who wanted to "get rid" of them.

I was shopping for a harness for our Boxer puppy (also a rescue), Lucy, in North Haven Petco. In the back of the store I heard a whimpering. I looked to see what the noise was and there were three puppies, in a shopping cart, no blanket, nothing. After looking around to find the "owner" of these puppies, I found no one. I went to the front cashier to ask if they knew of the puppies in the back of the store. They knew nothing. They paged on the overhead for the owner of the puppies to come forward. After 15 minutes, no one arrived. They had been abandoned.

One of the employees of the store had recalled these puppies from the weekend before, when a man was trying to sell them in front of the store.

I called my husband into the store, (he was waiting in the car with Lucy). He came into the store (with Lucy) and we knew we could not leave without finding the puppies a home. By that time I had made a big enough scene that two other people agreed to take the two females and we took the male.

We brought him directly to our vet and got him vaccinated and wormed—boy did he have worms!

Lucy loved him immediately and he even tried to suckle her (unsuccessfully). They instantly formed a bond and have been best friends ever since.

HONEY

THANKS TO AISLINN KERN

My husband and I have five girls. Three of them are two-legged biological children and the other two are four-legged furry pittie loves.

We rescued both of our dogs. Although they had never been abused, both were headed for the pound. I have some amazing photos of our girls together that would melt anyone's heart, especially our dog Honey and our daughter Lily.

Honey is our six-month old pit bull that we adopted this past summer when she was only ten weeks old. Lily is her four-year-old best friend and sister. Honey and Lily are truly inseparable.

BOCEPHUS AND DAISY

THANKS TO AMANDA CRITTENDON

Here are Bocephus and Daisy. Daisy is the one with more white on her. We got Daisy from a rescue because Bocephus was getting older and our Chihuahua was getting too small for him to play with. We looked at rescues from Lost But Loved (LBL) Rescue and found Daisy. She was a year old and surrendered because she had Parvo.

We first met at a dog park on neutral ground. She would not even look at me. I tried to walk her around but she just did not want to let the woman who brought her, out of her sight. So we met a week later at our house to see if she would get along with our daughter and our other pittie, Bocephus. Not even a minute after getting out of the car, she took to our daughter like she had known her for her whole life, and the same with Bocephus.

We got her the next week and she was so frightened that it took us three hours to even get her to come into our house. Now, she lets our daughters crawl all over her and lay on her. She sits on our laps because everyone knows all big dogs think they are lap dogs. She loves any kind of attention we give her. Daisy is a wonderful, wonderful dog, best friend and companion. We could not love her any more than we do.

GORDY

THANKS TO DENNIS FRAZIER

I adopted Gordy in San Bernardino, California. He is a blue nose pit bull that ended up back in the shelter for the second time. This time the owner did not return for him.

I am a truck driver and he goes with me on every trip I make. He has never met a person that he does not like and shows his love for people every day. He sleeps in the bed by my side and lays his head in my lap as I drive.

He gets along well with my other dogs. First up is Sam, a male pit bull, then Pearl, a female Rottweiler and Jed, another male pit bull. All of my dogs are rescued. Sam was roaming the streets of my hometown, Jed was found in Macon, Georgia and Gordy is from California. Pearl belonged to a friend that could no longer keep her, so I took her in.

There are a lot of stores I could tell you about Gordy, but mostly I want people to know he is a good boy and the most loving dog with the most loyal heart. He is my best friend.

QUINCY

THANKS TO SEANA MORRIS

This is the story of the most successful relationship I have had in my adult life.

Right before my biggest break up-or at least that is what I thought at the time. I decided to randomly peruse Petfinder. After only having had two family dogs and one of my own personal dogs at the age of 29, I felt compelled to have a pit bull. This decision came from not knowing a thing about the breed, but solely being in love with their eyes and how I considered them to be "human eyes."

From the few that I knew and the ones I constantly saw on the internet, they always felt so expressive and full of love.

I looked for about ten minutes, going through the alphabet from A-Z, reading about each of these sad souls just looking for a miracle. I was past the P's and into the Q's, and there was Quincy with big red letters reading: URGENT. He had been taken from a fighting ring in New York, born there, raised there, put into a shelter, fostered, adopted out and then when his adoptive family could not handle him, he was put out onto the streets of New York instead of being brought to anyone that could actually help him.

He was then found again but no one would adopt him. On top of this horrible start to life, he was born deaf. This was seemingly the hardest part for him, because he was an "over the top" 65-pound pit bull who had nothing but energy, no concept on how to use it and no one who would take the time to learn how to communicate with him. He literally had nothing.

Being a sucker for a cute face, I immediately contacted the rescue, which sadly is no longer. I set up a home evaluation and started reading about the breed so that when the rescue volunteers came to see where I lived, I would be seemingly educated on what I was getting into. Not the case, though! They came, they thought I was great, they placed him with me and one week later I was on my way to meet my main man Quincy, for the first time!

What a reality check that was! I cried for the first three weeks, not understanding him, trying desperately to train him the same way I had trained my yellow lab and failing miserably. I second-guessed my decision every night that I was home alone with him. Until one day, something just clicked and we started to really bond over "chuck-it." When we first started playing, he had no idea what a ball was, it took him a long time to warm up to the idea of chasing it. Now he knocks over anything in his way, especially if there is a tennis ball!

I started really researching deaf dogs and speaking to him using the commands that he responded to. We were finally getting through to each other! For weeks it felt like we were never going to have a relationship, that he would always be "pushing my buttons," until I started to tailor my training and communication. That made all the difference. From then on, we were inseparable! As my relationship came to an end, he stuck by my side. On the days I did not want to get out of bed, he made me play ball with him. When I did not feel like exercising, he made it apparent that he did. On nights that I just wanted to be alone, he forced his way to being the shoulder that I cried on.

We have moved three times since I first rescued him and each time he has taken on his new surroundings with confidence. He has been the sole reason I followed my passion and started a successful dog walking business in Boston, Massachusetts. He has been my biggest fan and the most loyal companion I have ever come across. He is, for all intents and purposes, my very best friend. My life would have never been such an adventure, a lesson, or a labor of love without him. He has become my "person," and I am thankful every day that he chose me. He truly saved my life just by being there.

LAYLA

THANKS TO GRADY AND LINDSEY ROUGHTON

We adopted an American Bulldog five years ago (from our local Humane Society) and she has absolutely been the best dog we have ever had. She was just five weeks old and has most certainly become a part of our family and is essentially one of our children.

Layla, was a little over two when our first daughter was born. She has been such a great dog since then as well. She is so much bigger than my daughter but she lets Caiden (our daughter) just fall all over her, laying on her, chasing her, whatever. Layla will play with Caiden, knows to be gentle and does an amazing job being careful with her.

Right after Caiden was born, Layla would not leave her side when we were at home. She constantly followed us wherever we were leaving Caiden and would just lie down nearby. To this day, she is very protective of Caiden. When we all take walks, Layla is constantly watching our surroundings and continuously places herself between Caiden and anyone or anything else.

It is truly amazing. Layla has been a blessing. She exercises and hikes with us, has helped to keep us in shape and keeps us all centered and grounded.

BUBBA

THANKS TO TRACEY PETRY

I live in Northford, Connecticut. This past May, I went to a shelter, traveling about thirty-five minutes to the Bridgeport Animal Shelter in Bridgeport, Connecticut to look for a dog. We had been looking at all the pit bulls and pit mixes when I walked into another building housing more dogs. While there I saw a big beautiful pit bull mix. He seemed to just speak to me. I felt like we had an immediate connection. I took him out for a walk and he was crazy on the leash. My husband wanted no part of this, but I fell head over heels with my Bubba. Now I had to leave without him and try to convince my husband that there are no bad dogs, just bad breeders.

Two weeks passed and I still wanted to bring Bubba home. Then Bubba's time was up. My friend Jenn and her daughter, who both rescue dogs, saw the last plea for Bubba, and they went to pull him. I was finally able to convince my husband to give Bubba a chance.

We have had him six months now and we also have a nine pound rescued Yorkie and a rescued half exotic Lynx cat. They all get along, and my husband and Bubba have become hopelessly attached. Bubba is a great dog, and very loyal to his Mommy for sure.

Because I took the time to educate myself, I was able to open my eyes and see how loving these dogs can be despite the harm that people have done to them.

ROXIE

THANKS TO CHRISTINA CUEVAS

This is my pit bull Roxie with her best friend Moca, (a Chihuahua). Finding them cuddling together as shown in the photo is an every-day occurrence. Both dogs have been devoted to each other from day one and are inseparable.

Both were rescues from Los Angeles shelters. When I found Roxie, she was very sick with an upper respiratory infection. She also had what appeared to be bedsores on all of her joints-as if she had been made to sit on concrete in the same position for weeks. She was so sick that she was deemed unable to undergo temperament testing, thus making her status unadoptable. She was set to be euthanized as soon as possible. Luckily, the United Hope for Animals Rescue was notified of her status and of the fact that I had previously expressed interest in her. Through this amazing rescue, I was able to save her before she was put down. I am so grateful that everything has worked out as it has and that both dogs have each other.

PART FOUR

JUST DOGS

"No matter how little money and how few possessions you own, having a dog makes you rich."

~ Louis Sabin

"Dogs have given us their absolute all. We are the center of their universe. We are the focus of their love and faith and trust. They serve us in return for scraps. It is without a doubt the best deal man has ever made."

~ Roger A. Caras

MEA

THANKS TO AMIE ARDITI

After I lost my sweet ninety pound pittie boy to cancer, I was beyond heartbroken. The only thing I could think of to help myself heal was to adopt another death row pit bull. I figured nothing could bring my boy back but maybe I could save another life in his name.

A month after my boy crossed the Rainbow Bridge, I did just that. I went to the Manhattan Animal Care Center in New York City, which is notorious for killing animals, and adopted my girl Mea. She was set for euthanasia but I was able to rescue her in time. She has brought me so much joy and has become my son's best friend.

My heart still hurts over my loss, but the love of a shelter pup is unlike any other. Mea seems to know she was saved, and she is forever grateful! It is a beautiful thing to be able to wake up each day and see her smiling face. There is no greater feeling in the world.

OLIVIA

THANKS TO MISTY ROSS

My husband and I rescued our pit mix Olivia, about six years ago when she was a one year old puppy, in Gainesville, Florida. My Beagle had just passed away and I just felt so empty without a dog, especially when getting out of the shower for some reason. My Beagle would always be waiting for me, just as Olivia does now. I was set on getting a male dog and one that was considered a "New Hope," meaning due to be euthanized within seventy-two hours.

Before he met me, my husband had never owned a dog but had two cats. However, he bonded with my former dog and was ready for another to fill the void. As we walked the aisles at the shelter, Olivia (then named Gaya) was one of the few who was not barking or jumping or even interested in us as we passed. We had taken a few other male dogs out and had almost settled on one when a volunteer came out and asked, "Have you seen Gaya?" to which we replied "no." Honestly, I knew that the dogs with more energy would be harder to adopt out so I had already decided to take a younger, more active dog. As it turned out, Gaya had been hit by a car and left on the road to die.

She had endured a broken hip and multiple internal injuries from which she was recovering. That explained why she was just lying in the corner of the kennel. Despite these injuries and recent surgeries, the moment we brought her out, she ran and played and began licking my husband in the face and ears. He was instantly in love and it was quite obvious that we were no longer in control of choosing our next pet—she chose us!

On paper, they had her breed as Fox Hound/Bulldog mix but I knew she was more likely a Pit Bull/Fox Hound mix. Unfortunately, due to the stereotypes surrounding the breed, this is a common occurrence to increase the dogs' chances of being adopted. Though my landlord was hesitant due to her 50-pound size, she reluctantly agreed to let us take Olivia home to our rental condo.

She has been a great addition to our family, despite the fact that we have to keep her separate from our cats, and I know that she is going to continue to be protective of us, as well as our new baby, who will arrive in February. I never thought I would own a pit bull, but now that I have, I will never have another breed of dog! She is so reliable, funny, smart, and loyal. A lap dog who thinks she is the size of a Chihuahua!

KAYNE

THANKS TO LAURA BIBBEE

I had never thought much about having a pit bull. I stuck to dependable breeds like Labradors because I have children. I already had two rescue dogs, a Lab mix and a Shepherd mix, so I was not in the market for a dog anyway. That was until one night on Facebook, a picture of a dog appeared on my newsfeed.

It was obviously an American Pit Bull Terrier. He was being shared by a rescue group as a last resort—his time was up the next day. The information said he had stopped eating and his picture told me he had shut down in the shelter.

What many people do not realize about pit bulls, and what I had not realized about them, is they are very much people dogs. They do not thrive without people—they just cannot. As soon as I saw this dog, I knew I was going to get him. I called all morning to the rescue and the shelter to let them know I would be there by late afternoon, so they would not put him down. It was a four hour drive but nothing was going to stop me.

When I picked him up, I had to carry him to the car because he would no longer walk on his own. He refused pepperoni rolls and lied still in my front seat the whole way home. Yet when we got home, and he saw my dogs and my kids, he got up. After his bath he ran to my son and sat in his lap. The next day he started to eat. My Kayne is the best dog I have. He loves to play with my kids, follows me everywhere, and has been easier to train than my other two dogs. He has tripled in size in just four months and is the sweetest dog in the world.

I never had a pit bull because of my kids. Now, I do not think twice about him playing with them because I know he would never hurt them. I know he would never let anyone else hurt them either. If I had it to do over, all I would ever own are pitties. They are a wonderful breed that has sadly been given a bad reputation because of the actions of bad owners.

BUDDY

THANKS TO HARRIET ELLS

I have a pit bull mix named Buddy.

I adopted him from the Yolo County SPCA in Davis, CA. Even though I live in Los Angeles, I drove the seven hours north because I fell in love with Buddy on Petfinder.

I already had a dog, Jimmy, who is an adult Shar Pei mix. He needed a pal. I was looking for a smaller female but ended up with Buddy—all 70 pounds of him.

One reason I was also attracted to him is because of his color. He is black, and I know that black dogs are often the last dogs left in the shelter.

Buddy was abandoned at a week old and was bottle-fed by his rescuers. I took him home when he was six months old. Since then
(he is two years old now), he has been a constant companion. He
is adorable and LOVES to cuddle but is still a bit skittish with loud
noises. He loves sitting next to me on the couch and sleeping at
the foot of my bed. He plays really well with Jimmy, although sometimes he does annoy his big brother by wanting to play too much!

BLAZE

THANKS TO NANCY

Before I decided to adopt Blaze, I had always been a cat person. I had never had a dog before because I never wanted a dog. I thought they were not very smart, annoying and a bit yucky. I shuddered at the thought of cleaning up dog poop and never understood how people could let their dogs lick their faces. I thought it was disgusting!

I did feel terribly about all the animals that are euthanized due to owner surrenders, the New York City Housing Authority (NYCHA) ban, excessive breeding and sadly, neglect and apathy. (For those of you not local, the NYCHA has a ban on dogs over twenty five pounds in their apartments.) I saw Blaze's picture on a Facebook page that I had been following, called "Urgent Part 2, Urgent

Death Row Dogs." It is a wonderful page that has led to the rescue of many homeless dogs.

I have always been the type of person to do something myself instead of waiting for someone else to do it. I did want to get him out. But there was one thing that I was ashamed of myself for. Something that kept me from going to get him: his breed.

Blaze is a pit bull mix. I had heard so many stories on the news about these vicious dogs. Hearing how they had locked jaws on a person, and could tear you to shreds and kill you. Yes, many of them are just stories. I stupidly believed the hype. I really wanted to get him out of the shelter but I was quite fearful. I was afraid for my cats' lives and even for my own life.

Even with all my apprehension and crazy ideas about the horrors of these monster dogs, I decided to face my fears. I went to the shelter to get Blaze to safety first thing in the morning. Unfortunately they do not start adoptions until noon. I persisted though, and went back during my lunch break.

I was not prepared for Blaze at all. I did not have the right leash, harness or collar, nor even a crate for him. What I did have were my ridiculous fears.

Thankfully, Blaze's Urgent family was there to help. I was offered money to buy a crate, which I did not accept. I was amazed that a complete stranger would make such a generous offer to help someone she did not even know. I was contacted by a few trainers. Harriet, who is one of the trainers at Red Hook Dog Rescue, even came to my place to assist me with Blaze. She gave me her personal phone number and was there for me for a few frantic situations. Had we not had Harriet on our side, Blaze would probably not be with us today.

By Blaze being a puppy, he had a few bad habits. He liked to play tug of war with the leash and also with my sleeve. The problem with him playing tug of war with my sleeve is that my arm is normally in my sleeve. One day while we were in the park, Blaze grabbed my sleeve and would not let go. My life flashed before my eyes and I thought all my fears were about to become reality - I was shaking. I was able to tie his chain to a fence and then got him to let go, but our walk was officially over.

I immediately called Harriet and told her what happened. She assured me that Blaze was playing. I believed her but I really started thinking about giving him up because I was scared that it would happen again. I did not want to risk him being put to sleep, so I decided against throwing in the towel. Instead of giving up, I decided to try extra hard to work it out with Blaze and make him the best dog that he could be.

The first thing I did was decide not to be afraid anymore, or Blaze would be the one controlling me. I read a training book that a kind woman from "Urgent Part 2" mailed to me. I looked up a lot of training videos on YouTube. I got really great treats and the proper harness. I had made a commitment by adopting Blaze and I was determined to do the best that I possibly could with him.

After a few weeks, I started to see results. Months later there was an enormous improvement. Blaze now knows how to sit and he gives handshakes and kisses on command. The newest trick he does is when I ask him, "Does your back itch?" he lays on his back and starts wiggling around and makes the funniest sounds. Every day he makes me laugh, and I smile just thinking about him.

Blaze has blossomed into a wonderful companion, goofball extraordinaire and my very best friend. Instead of being locked in a crate, Blaze sleeps next to me. If I am ever sad or upset, Blaze comes over to me and licks my face, and I let him. I actually even like it and I admit that at times I initiate the smooching. I do not mind picking up his poop, in fact I commend him and tell him what a good boy he is when he goes.

I have learned so many important lessons thanks to Blaze. One of those lessons is to not let fear keep me from doing what I want to do. I learned not to believe most of what the mainstream media presents as truth.

Another lesson is to never give up, no matter what. I have also learned to never judge a book by its cover. Pit bulls are simply dogs, like any other dogs, needing love, patience, time and proper guidance. They are a reflection of the way you treat them.

I would like to encourage anyone who has been contemplating adopting a dog to do it! It has been one of the best things I have ever done for myself. I love Blaze more than I could have imagined and I never get tired of looking at his adorable, expressive face and his super cute, floppy ears. I also use every opportunity possible to tell people that he is from a shelter and I always defend his breed.

I wish that everyone could experience what I have with Blaze. He has immensely improved my life and I want to say, "I love you Blaze!"

MATTIE

THANKS TO SARA LUNDBERG

My husband and I went to the local pound to look at a dog, and decided she was just not right for us. On the way out we saw a sweet pit bull but passed on her too, because we thought pit bulls were mean.

The next day I called my husband and asked him to go look at her again. We ended up taking her and named her Mattie. I was a little scared of her for a good few months because of all the negative things I had heard. I actually called my mom in tears the day we adopted her, thinking we had made a terrible mistake. But Mattie just continued to prove herself as the best, most rock solid dog I have ever had. She was very smart and her behavior was amazing.

Two years later I decided to foster, specifically to foster pit bulls because Mattie had gotten so along well with other dogs. I had grown to love the breed because of her. I had another positive experience when finding another dog on Petfinder. Despite being intimidated by the terrifying picture, I went anyway because this was the same city shelter I had gotten Mattie from. I found out this new dog was not so bad after all but there would be a few trials.

I took her out with some treats in my pocket and she was so eager to please. She already had "sit" down pat! When I got back to the gated kennel she realized what was happening and put on the brakes. I had only some crumbs in my pocket and attempted to toss them into the kennel but she was having none of it. I had to actually get behind her and push her butt to get her back in. I left in tears. I told my husband that I had to go and get her the next day or I would forever have the image of pushing that poor dog in my memory.

Her name is Stella and she has been with us now for 7 years. We unfortunately lost Mattie last December. Stella is just a sweetheart, a good dog right out of the box. She has never even jumped on or become aggressive with anyone!

We have started to foster again—only pit bulls that are rescued from the NYC system about to be euthanized. Thanks to Mattie I am now a huge pit bull advocate and fan, and am outright obsessed with them! Mattie truly changed my life!

BEECHER (AND SIBLINGS)

THANKS TO BRANDI BYERS

I have three pit bulls. I have never really thought about the breed but ended up taking them in because they were throwaways. Our first is named Blackjack. He is a pit/Mastiff mix. My son and husband were fishing one day when a skinny, mangy looking dog wandered up to them. Poor baby had a choke collar growing into his skin because it was so tight. He was starved and appeared to be left on his own. We loaded him into the car and never looked back. Today, he is a happy old man at the ripe old age of nine.

My husband drives a trash truck. Back in July he found a momma dog, a red nosed pit, tossed behind some trash cans and four puppies in a box in the trash. The mom and one baby died at the scene but my husband brought the other three back to our home. Sadly, we lost two more, but one kept fighting. Through an amazing vet, a blood transfusion and days and days of IV fluids and medicine, we were able to save him. His name is Beecher. Today Beecher is five months old and is thirty-five pounds of muscle and a holy terror- but he also has a few quiet moments. When we were fighting to save him he would just lay with his head on me, and at times would cry for his littermates. I think he still misses them, but he knows he is loved.

We got our last baby on Halloween. She was on death row and was scheduled to die that day. I agreed to foster her until a permanent home could be found. As soon as we got her home we knew she was special. She was a real love. She gave kisses like a pro. She would look at us as if asking permission before she would do even normal things like eat, drink or go potty. She did not know how to play and this broke our hearts.

She does everything in her power to make sure we are happy. Although it has only been a few weeks, we have watched this little lady grow. She is happy and is figuring out that she is loved. She plays and acts as a momma to Beecher the puppy. She still gives kisses with the best of them. Needless to say we really are not very good at this fostering thing!

MIDNIGHT

THANKS TO KAYDINCE DiNAPOLI DUPRE

This is Midnight. Midnight was not a traditional rescue, as he did not come from a shelter or a rescue group. Midnight was four months old and on Craigslist. I will never forget seeing him for the first time. He was so skinny, dirty, mistreated, half bald, and infested with fleas. He had shown signs of being beaten but still had the sweetest eyes I had ever seen.

We went out and bought him food and toys and took him home. He had no idea what toys even were and chose to play with a rock instead. Those first few weeks were a roller coaster as we got to know him and he got to know us. After two weeks, my partner Eric had to leave us and I had no idea what I was going to do. I was now alone with this little black puppy. During those thirty-four days, Midnight and I bonded. He became my rock. The one thing I could depend on through anything. He was no longer just my dog.

I came to realize that anything I gave to him he gave back to me a thousand times over. Midnight is the best boy that has ever walked the earth. He loves people and always greets us with an uncontrollable wiggle and a never-ending smile. Midnight adores other dogs, cats and even bunnies. He is so accepting toward all my foster dogs and takes each one under his wing.

There are not enough words to describe what a great dog Midnight is. I love all of my dogs the same but I have to say, Midnight is my heart. He holds the key to my soul. Midnight is my sunshine on a cloudy day, my light in the dark, my joy through the pain, my warmth in the cold, my truth when everything else feels like a lie, my reason when I am confused. Midnight has taught me more about love, loyalty and strength in the last three and a half years than any person has taught me in my whole life.

He might not have been a traditional rescue but he will always be my greatest save—the little black pit bull that changed my world. Midnight and I used to have a saying: "always only you and me." We have since changed it to "always only us," since we have added more dogs to our family. But in that place in my heart that belongs only to Midnight, it will forever be "always only you and me."

LEXUS

THANKS TO ANGEL GOFF

My dog's name is Lexus. She is a red nose American pit bull terrier that I found on Craigslist. Originally, I was not going to take her in but when I saw what kind of home she was living in, I knew I needed to get her out. The owner was reluctant to let us meet her at her house—we had to meet her at a McDonald's.

Lexus is really timid around other people and other dogs. We will never know what happened to her in her previous life but this dog has become my best friend and I would not give her up for anything. People give me dirty looks when I walk down the street with my pit bull but I do not really care. I am a proud pit bull mom and my hope is to one day start my own pit bull rescue. I gave a second chance to a dog that would never have had one. I love my Lexus—she is the best dog ever. I have had her for a year and it has been the best year of my life.

TESSA

THANKS TO NICOLE PIZZUTO

My boyfriend Mike rescued our dog Tessa from the Hi-Tor shelter in Pomona, New York, a no-kill shelter, almost four years ago.

Two pit bull puppies, about three months old, that the shelter had named Tara and Tessa, had been found running in a park with no collars or tags and brought to the shelter. They were in danger of being sent to another shelter where they might have been killed when Mike and his roommate happened to visit the shelter in hopes of adopting a dog.

Mike adopted the one named Tara. He had not planned to adopt a pit bull but as soon as he saw her he knew she needed him. He felt guilty about leaving her sister behind so he changed Tara's name to Tessa in honor of her sister. We later followed up to find out what had become of the original Tessa and the good news is, she was also adopted and now has a wonderful family. We have kept in contact with her owners and frequently exchange pictures.

Tessa was a little difficult at first but with training she blossomed. When she first came home, Tessa would not even go up the stairs by herself, but Mike worked with her on her training and it has paid off. Mike and I met, and Tessa now lives with both of us. She welcomed me into their lives with nothing but love.

What we love most about her is her sweet nature and her personality. Tessa is always smiling and always wants to cuddle. She loves to give affection as much as receive it and loves being outside, prancing around on her leash. She loves to play and loves other dogs.

Tessa loves everyone and when she goes for walks and is around babies and puppies, she walks ahead wanting to protect them. She attends holidays with the family just like any other dog.

Mike's favorite story is about Tessa meeting his cousin who has Cerebral Palsy. Most other dogs would bark at him but when he first met Tessa she just put her paws on his lap and licked him. Mike says he has never seen his cousin so happy.

Tessa has since been back to the Hi-Tor shelter where she and Mike first met, and is still a volunteer favorite. We wanted to share her story because Tessa is like any other dog – she just happens to be a pit bull. She is happy to have a home and people that love her and she gives that love back every day.

CHARLIE AND BANDIT

THANKS TO BRITTANY NASH

My husband and I were looking for a puppy. I was seven months pregnant and spent a lot of time at home alone, with my four-year-old, so we wanted a dog to keep us company. We decided on adoption from the SPCA instead of going to a breeder. Our intentions were to get a puppy. We went to the SPCA and took a look around. The first dog I saw was a ten-month-old blue pit bull named Charlie. I fell in love instantly!

He came to the SPCA as an owner-surrender because his family had no time for him. We adopted him the same day. When we got him home he was hyperactive but it was just because he was in a new environment. The very first time we left him alone we discovered he had severe separation anxiety. He tore our house apart from top to bottom. We learned he had spent most of his life in a cage. Needless to say when we left he had his own room that had nothing in it he could ruin. Now he is sixteen months old and his anxiety has subsided. He sleeps in our four-year old's room at night as his security blanket. He is the most loveable dog in the world. Our six-month-old son can lay on him and he never minds at all. We love our pit bull Charlie very much.

Recently, I received a phone call from my brother. He was trying to find a home for a puppy and time was of the essence. I agreed to foster him until we found him a forever home. He was a tiny underweight pit bull who we named Bandit. I learned that Bandit was used as a punching bag and a soccer ball. He had been starved and the only attention he got was negative. So we brought him in and gave him some TLC.

Now his weight is normal and he is very happy. Our home became his forever home. I did not trust anyone else with him after all he had been through. It breaks my heart that people can look at dogs and think they are unaffected by what happens to them, that they somehow lack feelings. My dogs are spoiled and happy and more loveable than any other dogs I have ever encountered. Yes, they are pit bulls and yes, the best dogs in the world! Even after being abused, they forgive!

LUCKY AND BELLA

THANKS TO BRANDY ALLEN

One day, several of my cousins were walking through the woods in Essex, Maryland when they saw a white and brown American Pit Bull Terrier tied to a tree, severely emaciated. Lucky was literally a skeleton of a dog. She may have survived a couple of days at most, before she passed. They cut the rope and walked her home. They took Lucky to the vet and got her checked out, and she became part of the family. Lucky was very energetic and happy once she got better. Despite her past, she loved everyone. No one would ever have guessed what she went through. Lucky lived to be 11 or 12. My cousins spoiled her, but we knew she was thankful to be with us.

My second story is about my baby girl Bella. I rescued Bella from a drug dealer. I got her when she was about four months old. She was emaciated like Lucky and looked even younger because she was so thin. Bella is a laid back, happy, and spoiled girl. She is very protective but is an amazing dog. My family knew nothing of this breed and we were afraid because of the way pit bulls are portrayed by people and the media. Lucky and Bella taught all of us that these dogs are nothing like that. We are all grateful that Lucky and Bella found us.

ZUKO

THANKS TO ROCCO D'URSO

In May of 2012 I was looking to adopt a dog. I had been to all of the shelters in my area and found a lot of good candidates, but none that I truly felt was my match. I was never allowed to have a dog when I was living at my parents' home. Now, since I own my own home with a large enough backyard, I thought ok, now was the time.

I was on Facebook when I saw a post from the Waterbury animal shelter for Rocco the blue nose pit bull. He was my namesake! I knew I had to meet him. I called to make sure he was still available and he was! When I arrived, he calmly walked down the hallway towards me, instantly locking eyes. I sat on the curb to allow him to sniff and acclimate himself. He let out a sigh, relaxed his head on my lap and lied down. I said to the shelter volunteer, "Give me the paperwork, he is coming home with me."

I knew of the terrible things people say about pit bulls, but there was no doubt in my mind he was nothing but a gentle creature. I had to change his name because having two Roccos in the house would be too confusing. So I named him Zuko, after Danny Zuko from Grease.

From what the shelter knew of him, he was found lying on the steps in front of a building in Waterbury, left to suffer. I immediately scheduled an appointment to have all of his tests done and to have him neutered. Zuko had a parasite infestation and the vet also found a large hernia just above his genitals. He offered to remove it while he was performing the neuter procedure. After a couple of emergency vet visits for his popped stitches, Zuko healed completely and had become a lot more active and playful—like a completely different dog.

When I adopted him he was at sixty pounds. He is now over seventy-five pounds and still thinks he is a lap dog. He wants nothing but to cuddle and give you kisses. We now have an eight month old named Rocco Francesco. So much for not having too many Roccos! Rocco and Zuko are the best of friends. Zuko is so gentle and very protective. Rocco cannot stop staring at Zuko and every time he passes, Rocco stretches his hands out trying to pet Zuko. He has a smile on his face every time he sees Zuko.

Although Zuko was a large investment, he was worth every penny. He is the best, sweetest dog I have ever met. All he wants is love. He is a great big brother to Rocco and I cannot wait for them to grow up together.

I love to take Zuko out wherever we go. Although there are times I get very angry at the ignorance people have towards pit bulls. I will not mention the name of the pet store I took Zuko to. We were going to pick out some new toys. There was an adoption event going on and 4 of the 5 volunteers that were there saw Zuko and instantly picked up the smaller dogs, as if they needed protection from Zuko. They said to me, "Oh it's not that we are afraid of you, these little dogs will tear him apart." If that were true, I wondered why they were trying to adopt them out to children if they were that aggressive.

As we walked further into the store, there were children in pens with other dogs playing with them. The dogs in the cages began to bark at Zuko, and Zuko just sat with his tail between his legs because he is very submissive. One of the volunteers approached me and made a statement that it was possible that my dog's presence in the store might be upsetting, provoking the other dogs. Basically, they wanted Zuko and me to leave the store. I guess the ignorance will always be there. I call it the racism of a breed, just as there is still racism amongst human cultures to this day.

We can only try to educate the ignorant but it is aggravating and offensive whenever someone singles out our pit bulls because of their breed. I have spoken to a lot of fearful people but Zuko has converted many of them into believers that it is not the breed, but the owner. People that were absolutely terrified and in tears saw that my son was next to him and figured, "Hey, he is with a baby, how bad could he be?" They actually thanked us for showing them how truly loving and harmless these dogs can be.

There is nothing better than the appreciation you get from an animal that gets a second chance. They are truly appreciative of the new life they are given. Just ask Zuko (Rocco)!

TIFFANY (AND CHARLIE)

THANKS TO JEROMY McFARREN

I live in Schuylerville, New York, in Saratoga County, near Saratoga Springs.

I had gotten a pit bull/ boxer mix as a puppy from a girl whose pit bull recently had puppies. I had him (Charlie) for about four years, when I was at the mall one day. Charlie was always a good dog. He was and is, a loving and sweet energetic boy. I thought that I would probably get another dog at some point as a friend for him. I figured I would get a small dog but I had no definite plans. It was all pretty abstract.

As I was shopping that day I heard barking in the mall and noticed that the Saratoga County Animal Shelter had some tables set up. I walked over to their table and started looking at the pamphlets and other things that were displayed about their facility and their animals. While reviewing some of the materials presented, I felt a wet nose in my hand and looked down to see this red nosed pit bull looking up at me. She was shaking her whole body as she licked my palm. She was a sight to see. They had her wearing pink sparkly fairy wings, a pink sparkly crown and a tutu. Her wings were askew and her crown was tipped to the side. I knelt down to pet her and she licked my face.

The women running the booth told me that her name was Tiffany and that she had been at the shelter for seven months, picked up as a stray. When they found her, she had on a collar that basically had a choke-hold her. This resulted in a loss of hair at the back of her neck, which is now scarred over. She will never grow hair on that spot. They said she was generally wary of men, but that she was a sweet girl and one of their favorites. As I talked to the women I watched Tiffany as she sniffed and kissed people that happened to come near her. She was obviously liked by everyone that came near her. For some reason, I could not leave the area. I had looked at puppies and other dogs at adoption clinics before and was always able to resist any urge to take one home. But something was different here. I could not leave there without her.

I must have stood there watching her for about twenty minutes or more. She would periodically return to me and look at me with her soulful brown eyes and lick my hand and face. I noticed that she walked a little funny and was told that her back legs were not so good. She had noticeable scars on all of her legs.

I could not understand how such a sweet girl could be at the shelter for seven months! It is true, she had some medical issues and she was about three or four years old. I guess people want an animal they will not have to give a lot of attention to, who knows? The women at the booth told me that the adoption fee for Tiffany was only twenty-eight dollars. I could not believe that. The dogs at other adoption fairs had been upwards of three hundred dollars. The decision was made. I would take her out of there.

I was a little worried about how Charlie would be with her, but more importantly, how she would be with him. Charlie was my baby boy, the love of my life, and I wanted him to be safe. They assured me that if it did not work out between the two of them that I could bring her back. So I brought her home, and they were wary of each other at first. Initially, I was so nervous, thinking I had made a mistake. I actually contemplated bringing her back. But I decided to wait and see how it would go. That night I cried a little, thinking that Charlie might think I was replacing him. The next day, we all went for a morning walk together, and they were fine.

Later that year, after a visit to the vet with Tiffany, it was decided that she needed to have surgery on her eyelids. They were rolling inward and causing ulcers on her eyelids. By that time I had completely fallen in love with Tiffy, (as I now referred to her). She was so sweet and loving. Always by my side, she affectionately kissed Charlie and licked him as if he was her puppy. I dropped her off at the vet's office one morning to have her eyes fixed and felt a nervous heaviness in my chest. I wondered if she might think I was abandoning her at another shelter. The thought of that broke my heart and I could not wait to get back there in the evening to pick her up.

When it was time, I waited for her to come out, hoping she would be relieved to see me. Her eyes were stitched up all around, making her look like a Halloween fright. She was unsteady from the anesthesia, but wagged her tail when she heard me calling to her. I could barely contain myself as we drove the short distance home. But when we got there, walking her to the house, I began to sob uncontrollably. I knew she would feel better afterwards. However, the emotion of her not knowing where she was going and what was going to happen to her filled me up with grief. I hugged her and kissed her head and told her I loved her.

She healed up nicely though. Her routine now consists of having two different eye drops administered. This will have to be the case for her, for the rest of her life. She never resists her treatments and always gives me kisses afterwards. Recently she has begun to show signs of arthritis in her back legs and has a tough time in the cold months. She is well known at the vet's office and they say she is one of their favorite dogs because she is always so sweet and gentle. My own heart fills with more love every day for her. I can honestly say that adopting her was the best thing I have ever done as a human being.

By having dogs I have learned how to love. I believe that pit bulls, especially those that have been abused or neglected, are excellent teachers about what it means to love. Their capacity to trust is immense, despite what may have happened to them. Tiffy had obviously been neglected, if not worse. Then to be a stray and spend seven months in a shelter must have been lonely and depressing. When I adopted her I made the commitment to care for her for the rest of her life and I will. She is home now and I could never give her up for anything.

SMOKEY (FKA ET)

THANKS TO SALLEE HANNON

We adopted an abused pit bull after he had nowhere to go. We never thought we would own a pit bull since my husband was once attacked by one. Our dog Muffin died a year ago and we missed having a dog in our lives. Then we saw a tiny, sad dog online and I knew he needed us. He was a pit bull. With my husband's past trauma, he was not so sure if this was a good idea.

When ET, (named because of his big head and small body) came home, he could not walk, had not known what it was to play, or do anything a dog does. We decided to change his name to Smokey because of his beautiful gray color. It took weeks of love and patience for us to help him. Now, almost three months later, he is doing extremely well. He is almost 35 pounds, loves to go for walks and has plenty of clothing and toys to keep him occupied. Smokey is pure love and knows he was saved—he knows.

KAPPA

THANKS TO PAT MIGLIORE

When my son was in university, he joined a frat house and soon after, they got Kappa as a puppy (hence, her name). She was the runt of her litter. My son fell in love with her since he had always wanted a dog. She lived in his room but belonged to the frat. So he got his own puppy, a male that he named Zeppelin. For two years, Zeppelin and Kappa lived in my son's room. The day came when my son graduated, left the frat house and had to leave Kappa behind. From time to time he would return but as time went on, he saw Kappa become more and more depressed from the constant revolving door of people in and out of her life.

Fast forward five years and the frat began to recognize that she was not dealing well with the constant change and felt it was in her best interest to get a new home. My son could not take her. He still had Zeppelin and had since adopted another dog from a kill shelter. He felt that two dogs were as much as he could handle. I am sure you know what happened next.

First I said, "No." I had not had a dog in all my adult life even though I had one as a child. My husband, on the other hand, had never had a dog. And while we are not retired, we do have an empty nest and can pretty much come and go as we please. Our next option was to consider a big "maybe"—with the intention of taking her for my son's sake, so that she would not leave his life completely.

We took her for a trial weekend. For the first 24 hours, she behaved like a well-mannered house guest. Then I sat down on the couch, she climbed up beside me and laid her head in my lap. That was it. I was not letting her go anywhere else after that.

Likewise, my husband fell madly in love with her and now she is our baby girl. So much of it is a credit to her. She is as sweet as can be and very adaptable. Because of all the people that came through the frat house, she is extremely well socialized. We can take her almost anywhere with us and she fits in well with the things we like to do. We take her hiking and when we go antiquing, she waits in the car (provided that the weather is okay). She is well behaved and I built a stronger foundation by working with my good friend who is a dog trainer.

We are constantly being complimented on her calm behavior, friendliness and good manners. Because she has a longer, more tapered muzzle, people often think she is a pit bull mix. I am constantly amused at people that are petting her, complimenting us for her demeanor saying, "You know this girl has a bit of pit in her, don't you?" Then I tell them she is full, 100% pit.

Because I was not sure about her experience with small children, I took that cautiously at first. While we do not have any little ones in the family, when we are out and about, with extended family or when we are coming in and out of our condo at the shore, she encounters them. She sits quietly and patiently with children as they swarm over her. If she has had enough, she simply walks away and finds a corner away from them.

Our situation at home is also beneficial to her. We have a large fenced in yard and I work from home. In the past six months, she has spent more time outside than she probably has in her previous six years and is showing all the benefits of her new life. She is happy and contented. Pit bulls are fabulous dogs.

FLASH

THANKS TO BETSY FURST

My family and I are the proud owners of a pit bull named Flash. Two years ago, my then seven-year-old daughter and I were at the Post Mall in Milford, Connecticut. We were only there to use a gift card she had received for the holidays. I despise shopping in malls and was not thrilled to be there.

As we were walking out we noticed a young man with a puppy in a backpack. He was carrying the puppy in front as you would a baby in a carrier. We went over to admire the puppy. I asked what kind of dog he was. The young man said he was a blue nose pit bull and was looking for a good home for him. He also said that we were the first decent people to inquire about him.

I took out my phone and took a picture of Flash. I asked how much money he wanted and he said that he did not want money—just a good home for his dog. I tried to phone my husband, but he did not answer. This was a decision I had to make on my own. With my daughter jumping up and down, begging and pleading, I did what any mother would do, I said yes!

An hour later, we were driving home with our new puppy. It was meant to be! He is amazing and the best puppy we have ever owned.

You have to appreciate how impulsive this was on my part. We already had a dog at home, but Annie, our black Lab, welcomed Flash and they soon became like mother and child.

Last week we had to put Annie down after twelve wonderful years. We miss her terribly and we know Flash does too. Today, I was looking on pit bull rescues sites. I will never own another breed.

STELLA

THANKS TO PAULA DILLON

We became empty nesters. Kids out of the house and our beloved yellow lab dog of fifteen years had passed. We thought, now we have that freedom to come and go, take weekend getaways, and have no one to worry about at home. About a year went by and my husband (Joe) and I were feeling that sense of quietness, lack of life and activity in the home.

We talked about—maybe—adopting a dog. Joe had been perusing Petfinder. One day he showed me a picture of this cute, serious-looking, dog sitting in a little dog bed that actually belonged to her Jack Russell foster brother. The dog was advertised as an American Bulldog mix. So, Joe called about the dog. Her foster mom, Deidre, had named her Arwen.

Deidre brought Arwen over the next day and left her for a short time. When Deidre left, the dog jumped up on the couch, looked out the window and howled watching her foster mom drive away. It was heartbreaking, but I also saw this as a positive sign. This dog had a lot of love to give and needed love. I could do that.

So, Arwen came home to us and was renamed Stella.

I started learning more about our new dog. I learned that she is a pit bull. Call me ignorant, but I did not think she was a pit bull. My belief was that a pit bull was a dog that had a scary looking face, baring its teeth—we all know the negative media portrayal. So now this pit bull was living in my house, in my suburban family neighborhood in Cheshire and I was asking myself, "What did I do?"

We began acclimation of this new dog. I was sure this would never work. Stella met our cat, Lulu, and the chase began. I was sure Stella would kill my cat. Taking Stella for a walk brought me to tears every day. I wanted a dog so we could walk together. She was walking me, pulling my arm and not listening to anything I said.

Panicking, I called Deidre, to tell her what happened. I thought I had one of those terribly vicious pit bulls that would attack people like we read about in the papers. This was not what I had signed up for. Every day Joe and I said, "Okay, we should bring her back—we are the wrong owners for her." But she stayed. I felt like a failure. Deidre suggested we keep her on a temporary basis and see how we felt in a few weeks. We agreed.

I started researching more about the responsibility that comes along with owning a pit bull, the need to have a dog that would be well behaved and give the breed a good name. I was overwhelmed, and did not think I could do it. I wanted to like this new dog that had come to live with us, but I was regretting my decision. I do know that much of my apprehension was a direct result of her breed.

My husband and I worked on being good pack leaders. We did a lot of those little things that made all the difference over a period of time. We walked through the door first, invited her on the couch (although now she owns it, but we love her there now). I do not leave her unattended outside and practice walking her on a leash diligently, reinforcing good behavior versus punishing bad behavior. I must admit I spent a great deal of time with my girl. But oh, it was so worth it.

This March we will have had Stella for two years. Stella has taught me more than I could ever imagine. As they say, she has rescued me. I love her so much, feel so proud of where she is now, and miss her when I am not with her. She loves, appreciates and gives the best hugs and kisses, even to the cat.

When Stella first came home she was most comfortable in her crate, and never barked, whimpered, or really showed any affection. She did not wag her tail when we came home, or much at all. We thought she might be hearing impaired, because she was so flat with her responses. But, now this girl wiggles so much that I do not know how she has avoided breaking in half. Her tail wags incessantly and you better make sure it does not knock something over. Now, she only goes in her crate when we ask to her to. She sleeps like a pile of love in our bed with us and the cat.

Stella is far from perfect, but she is to me. I am very cautious with her meeting other dogs, because she has taught me that I must learn what is important to her. She must feel safe. She has her dog friends, but she taught me that all dogs do not have to be her friend. She loves when we have visitors to the house. Her bark is there, letting us know that someone is coming. If we say it is okay, she is a happy camper. She no longer jumps back in fear when people lean over her. She may possibly jump up for a kiss, but listens quickly and will sit nicely when asked. She is smart, wants to please and is so content having a warm sunny spot on a lounge chair outside or on the couch with her head resting on a lap.

Stella is my walking buddy, my devoted friend and companion. She helps me stay motivated to be outside every day so we both get our exercise. She loves my sons and I never worry about how she will act towards people that treat her appropriately and with respect. Her kindness to children is gentle and sweet. We bring her to see grandma at the convalescent home and grandma smiles. We also enjoyed Pit Bull Appreciation Day this year. She did great!

Now, I walk Stella proudly and when people ask me what kind of dog is she, I am happy and proud to say she is a pit bull. Sometimes people walk to the other side of the trail, but most people are happy to meet Stella and give her a friendly pat on the head or a treat, which she will always gladly accept.

As Cesar Milan always says: "You may not get the dog you want, but you will get the dog you need."

JAVA

THANKS TO TANYA DENNING

My husband (boyfriend at the time) had two pits, one male, and the other female. Well, you can figure out what happened next. Baby, the female, got pregnant and when she went into labor she delivered only one puppy that night. The next day she delivered four more–all stillborn. Sadly, she died giving birth. My husband brought the first puppy in the house and told me we had a problem. We went and purchased puppy bottles and formula. I bottle-fed this puppy, but my husband said not to get attached because she probably would not survive. He was wrong. My oldest grand-daughter grew up with her. The dog's name is Java. She is now four, weighs about 70 pounds, and will sit in your lap and suck on your ear. She is the biggest baby you will ever see. I love that dog!

KOOL AID

THANKS TO KATHI WHEELER

My little girl is the sweetest. The children in our neighborhood come to our house all the time and ask us if KoolAid can come out and play. KoolAid is our five-year-old pit bull. We rescued her from a shelter in Oregon four years ago.

I had heard all the stories and before adopting KoolAid, I read everything I could get my hands on about pit bulls. I also talked to the folks at Bad Rap Pit Bull Rescue in San Francisco. I then decided I could handle this breed. I will never go back. This is an amazing breed and KoolAid proves it every day!

PAIGE

THANKS TO STEPHANIE SLATER

I adopted Paige, a pit bull puppy, when she was four months old from the Connecticut Humane Society in Newington. She was rescued along with her momma and siblings from an abandoned house. They were covered in feces and filth.

She was timid at first but with the help of my older pit bull, Lovie, she quickly bounced back - literally! She hops like a bunny, gallops around, and her tail is always wagging. Paige is very loyal to her pack here and her love is unconditional. She is always happy to see her family! Paige is now 15 months old.

COLBY

THANKS TO MELISSA McCROHAN

About three years ago my husband and I decided that we wanted to add a dog to our family. We talked about what kind of dog we wanted, but neither of us wanted a pit. We had heard too many bad stories, and had young children to be concerned about.

We browsed page after page of adoptable pets, never seeing any that seemed like the right fit. We happened to stumble across All for Dogs Rescue on Petfinder, and there was Colby Jack, listed as a Staffordshire Terrier. He immediately caught us both. His classic pittie smile and the way he was laying with his legs splayed out behind him were clinchers. At that time, we did not even realize that Staffies were pit bulls. The only dog I had seen that I knew for certain was a pit was brindle, and Colby Jack is white and red. That is how uneducated about the breed I was.

We filled out an application and talked to people from the rescue group. He had started life as a rescue dog and been adopted by a young man. However, that young man entered the military and could not keep the dog, so back to rescue he went. We were told that Colby puts his "worst foot forward" when he meets someone because he is just so happy that he cannot contain himself. On the positive side, he had great house manners and loves to go on walks and play. He was in a foster home with other dogs and got along great with everyone.

It was decided that my husband would take the drive to meet him in person. It is more than a three-hour drive each way to where he was located (Bend, Oregon), but that did not deter us. My husband said as soon as he saw Colby in person for the first time he instantly knew this was his dog and that he was coming home with him. The kids and I could not wait for them to get home. Talk about a long day!

Once he arrived home, I was somewhat intimidated by him. He was totally adorable, but he had this big head and looked larger than what I expected. I was so careful with letting my young girls pet him and be around him, not knowing exactly how he would react. Later that night when the kids were in bed, I sat on the couch to watch some TV. Colby walked over to me and just stared. Then he put one paw up on my lap, then the other. Next thing I knew, this 50-pound dog was on my lap with his head in the crook of my arm and was fast asleep. And it was love!

Fast-forward to today and you will see a dog that is truly a member of the family. My girls cuddle with him, cover him with blankets, play with him, talk to him, etc. We take him on walks or to the mountains so he can endlessly chase sticks or play in the snow. He goes pretty much everywhere with us. He sleeps on our bed most nights—well, mostly my side. I have a heated blanket and he really likes that. And yes, he still puts his "worst foot forward" when meeting new people, but that is part of what everyone loves about him. You know when you come to our house that Colby will greet you with a smile and a kiss. He is just a happy dog. You cannot stifle that.

I do my best to be a positive advocate for the breed. Anytime we are in a park or out on a walk and someone talks to me about him I always tell them that he is an amazing dog. I also encourage people not to believe negative stereotypes associated with pits because it is mostly misinformation. I have found that anyone who has had a pit bull loves them. It is only the people who have never been around them that are afraid of them. My husband and I both agree it is "pits for life" for us, and rescue ones at that—adopt, do not shop!

MACIE

THANKS TO BRITTNIE

I adopted a four-month-old pit bull puppy about two months ago! My grandma was hesitant, as she had heard horror stories about this breed. I convinced her to meet my puppy, now named Macie. Macie is the most fun-loving dog we have ever met. She is either at play, sleeps, cuddles, or is giving kisses. Macie is the light of my life and even the people that seem to not like pit bulls say she is sweet!

COCO AND SOPHIE

THANKS TO JOYCE STEVENSON

My husband passed away six years ago. About six months after that a pit bull puppy came into my life. She was only about five weeks old. I found her under a chair on my porch. I was deathly afraid of pit bulls because of the way they were stereotyped. My son talked me into bringing her into my home and my life.

She was never claimed by anyone. I thought maybe my husband sent her to me so I kept her. We named her Coco. As it ended up, she has been an answer to my prayers. I live alone with my daughter. She became our protector and part of our family. Never in my life have I had a better dog.

She is so smart and well behaved, I just love her. One did not seem to be enough for me. So about three years ago, I decided to adopt another pit bull from a shelter in Chicago called Lucky Dog Rescue. Her name is Sophie. She also became a part of our family. I could not have asked for two better dogs! They have touched my heart so much that I advocate for pit bulls on Facebook. It is my way of giving back to the rescue dogs. The message: They are not broken. I am proud to have them by my side!

BUDDY

THANKS TO CAITLYN DALTON

Buddy was found with his mom and nine other brothers and sisters. The mom was very sick so she had to be separated from her pups and was put on medication to save her life. I took the puppies and bottle fed them until they could be placed into foster homes. Buddy and his sister May stayed with us as fosters. Buddy ended up staying with us permanently.

Buddy is a beautiful fawn colored pit bull who is the biggest baby you will ever meet. He cries if there is no room on the couch, he sucks on a blanket, and sits on your lap as if he is a ten pound dog. In reality, he is an eighty pound pit bull, but my family and I do not care at all. He has the biggest heart of gold. When I have fosters, (I mostly bottle feed puppies or kittens), he will take them under his wing. He will just lay there as they tug on his ankles or ears or jump on top of him. He never moves, and never snaps at them. He will lick them and play with them when they are big enough. I call him the animal ambassador of the household. We always have other dogs over for play dates or visits and Buddy is the first to say "hi". He loves to hike, swim, run, and play all day.

There is something about him. Almost a sixth sense, like he knows when someone is sick or is in trouble. When I came down with the flu, he was crying outside my bedroom door to get in. He jumped on the door, turned the handle, ran inside then jumped on the bed. He lied down next to me and did not move from my side until I felt better. Another time I took him to a friend's house to swim. I jumped in the pool and stayed under water to see what he would do. I was not really surprised with what happened next–he jumped head first into the water. He started swimming in circles above me then tried to dive down to get me. He was whining to alert the people around us. Never has he become so frantic when we have gone swimming in times past. Normally he will swim up to me and then let me hold him while he floats there and relaxes. I can truly say that I would trust this dog with my life.

Animals in general, are what owners make them. Yes, pit bulls have a lot of power, but they have even more heart. Back in the day, pit bulls were called "the nanny dogs" because of their amazing patience with kids, and I believe it. My Buddy, nannies my foster kittens and makes them trust dogs. We can learn a lot from our dogs, and I am so happy to have my pittie in my life to teach me new things every day.

BRIDGET

THANKS TO FRANCES CARVALHO

Adopting a pit bull changes everything. I have always had dogs and they were all special. Although I said, "No more dogs" after my last dog passed away, I was just looking online and Bridget's picture and short bio came up. I was in love.

I pestered Angel Capone Pit Bull Rescue in Connecticut until they gave me Bridget's foster's contact information. I then pestered Bridget's foster mom Sue. I finally convinced both I was worthy. I cannot believe I thought I knew dogs. I was neither worthy nor knowledgeable about having a rescue pit. I adopted Bridget and she has taught me about the breed.

Pit bulls are tenacious about what they want while loving you more than words could ever express. You go into a whole different world when you rescue a pit. You become involved in wanting to save this breed and dispel all the bad information. Bridget has a sad story as do most rescues but she will live out her life in peace with me. I am moving soon and my plan is to foster pit bulls in my new home. This is something I never even thought about doing before Bridget. These dogs have huge hearts and deserve a chance.

SOLDIER

THANKS TO HEATHER KOHLER

I am 40 years old and had only one dog my entire life. I was always nervous to get another dog. Every now and then I would consider it but I would never commit. Then a friend who owns an indoor dog park/boarding facility and another friend began rescuing pit bulls from a high kill shelter in Philadelphia.

Again I saw these adorable, lovable dogs, but was nervous and scared to jump in. I also found out I was deploying in 2014, so I was torn between living my life to the fullest, and being unfair to a dog by bringing it into our home, knowing I would have to leave soon.

In late May there was a Facebook post about two dogs and one was named Soldier. I had to inquire about Soldier. My rescue friends thought I was perfect for this dog. Soldier was having issues with other animals but was awesome with kids and people.

I met soldier on May 31, 2013, and that evening my son met him. We fell in love and Soldier Boy has been the light of our lives ever since. He is our 60-pound lap dog. He loves to hug and take walks. He has his moments from time to time but all he needs to do is flash that pittie smile and I melt. He has been a wonderful addition to our family.

OPIE

THANKS TO JOE NELSON

My story starts in Kalamazoo, Michigan. My brother was a manager at a local Pizza Hut. One day some customers complained that there was a pit bull outside and that they refused to leave the restaurant until the dog was removed. My brother went to investigate and found a malnourished pit bull tied to a bike rack with nothing but a keychain lanyard cut in half. He took one look at him and knew there was nothing vicious about him, with his big red nose and sad brown eyes. He was more than 20 pounds underweight with his ribs sticking out, yet somebody had taken the time to professionally crop his ears.

The Pizza Hut crew fed him and gave him water for the next four hours to see if someone would come to claim him but no one did, so Animal Control was called. My brother got the call 30 days later that no one had claimed Opie yet, and that he would be euthanized the next day at noon.

They were throwing out a lifeline, hoping that maybe my brother would want to pick him up because they had fallen in love with him too–and he did! The next day, even though he was just a broke college kid going to Western Michigan University, he rescued him. My brother kept him for a few months but realized he did not have the time or money to own a dog, so my girlfriend and I decided we would give him a chance and brought into our home.

After Opie was with us for a couple of months I woke up one morning to my girlfriend yelling, "He caught something!" and a horrific shriek was coming from the backyard. Not knowing what was going on and having a new dog, I did not know what to expect. As I ran into the backyard I found a rabbit stuck in my chain link fence and Opie standing over him licking his hindquarters. First of all, this showed us another positive side of our pit. Second, I never knew a rabbit could scream!

I called Opie over to me and he came running, the rabbit managed to back out of the fence and slide under the gate. His whole back half completely wet with saliva from getting licked by the dog! I have had dogs my whole life, but this is my first pit. He has been with us for over a year now and is one of the best dogs I have ever known!

BENTLEY

THANKS TO JEFF STATHAM

My first ever foster dog turned into my first foster failure. Bentley was picked up as a stray and his collar was embedded in his neck. Someone had cared for him at some point because he had previous hip surgery. He is one of five rescues in my home, and both my parents and my sister all say if they were to take one of my five pups, he would be it!

KYRA

THANKS TO LEA ERVIN

I consider my beautiful Kyra to be a rescue because if I had not taken her, I do not know what would have happened to her. My son and his fiancée got her when she was very young. I was not thrilled that they chose a pit bull because I was very uneducated about the breed back then. My reaction was like many unfamiliar with pits - I was truly terrified of them. My brother worked for the local gas company and had many bad experiences with them, which he of course shared with us. She seemed like a sweet puppy but I kept my distance because of all the terrible stories I had heard.

When she was almost eight months old, my son's fiancée passed away and he had to move out of their apartment. She was shuffled around for a few months, from place to place, but nothing seemed to work out. She would escape, or was not wanted, etc. My son came to me and asked me to please take her, (he knew I had a fenced in yard and could provide a safe place for her). He had already lost so much, I did not have the heart to tell him no.

He brought her to me a little over five years ago. I remember it like it was yesterday. She was so skinny, but such a happy girl. I had no plans of making her an inside dog at first, but by the second night she was sleeping with me in my bed. The plan was not to allow her on the furniture or the bed, so I put a big blanket on the floor right next to my bed. It went pretty well that first night. I ended up not sleeping much because I kept checking on her. She slept very well. I think maybe she knew she was finally home! That morning though, while I was taking a shower to get ready for work, she curled up on the couch like she belonged there. When I walked in to the living room she looked up at me with her beautiful eyes- and that was that. She is now allowed on all of the furniture, the beds, anywhere she wants to go.

She is the most amazing dog I have ever been around. I am so very blessed to have her in my life. My friends now all think I am the crazy dog lady. I have volunteered at a local pit bull rescue group and work very hard to be a good pit guardian. There was a Petsmart that opened up in our neighborhood just a few days after I got her. I knew they allowed dogs in the store and offered training programs. I called them and was very lucky to reach one of the trainers very familiar with pits. Kyra has now been through all levels at Petsmart, and someday I want to get her Canine Good Citizen Certification.

I also found out what an excellent job my son had done of socializing her when she was very young. Kyra loves everyone–kids, teenagers, adults, and seniors. She loves them all. She loves to give kisses and goofy smiles. I do always try to make sure the kids know to never approach a strange dog like they sometimes do, but luckily

Kyra is great about it. Sometimes the parents know she is a pit and they are fine with it. There are other times when some are fearful of her. We try to work with those people a bit to let them see just how awesome she is.

I usually tell them my story, about how I was scared at first too, until I became educated and was able to experience their true nature for myself. Sometimes the parents have no idea what kind of dog she is. I have actually had little gray-haired old ladies grab their kids/pups and scream, running away from us when they found out she was a pit. Inside, this just infuriates me, but I do try very hard to keep a polite and respectful demeanor towards them. We have changed many, many minds about the breed, this being one of my proudest accomplishments each time we do - one person at a time.

COCO

THANKS TO TAMMY CONNELLY

My husband and I adopted a pit bull from the Manchester, Connecticut pound almost two years ago. Her name is Coco and she is a diamond in the rough. An absolute gem! We live in South Windsor, Connecticut and for fifty dollars, we received a lifetime friend.

Coco will be three in January and is working towards becoming a therapy dog. She is extremely sweet, loves to cuddle and does not have a mean bone in her body. She loves all humans and all dogs. She goes to day camp once a week and loves to play with the other dogs. She has completed two levels of dog training and knows all basic commands. She has been wonderful around small children too.

We recently brought in a foster dog and she has been an amazing big foster sister. She continues to display such qualities as love and patience, along with being a good protector.

She really is an ambassador for the pit bull breed.

DIAMOND, ZOEY AND NATAS

THANKS TO JAMIE HARRIS

In 2003 my husband wanted to look at some Staffordshire puppies. I went with him and out came all these puppies. I think there were about nine or so, and they were only four and a half weeks old. All migrated downstairs away from us, except one little black fur ball. She was so shy yet curious, and had a beautiful puppy face that just broke my heart. I had to have her, so she was mine! In the car I noticed the white on her chest and the almost perfect diamond on the back of her neck. My daughter who was about four at the time had no clue that we were coming home with a puppy and I did not know the breed until we stopped off at the pet store. As we got into the car with all the goodies my husband said to me, "By the way, I may have told a little lie. She is a pit bull."

My jaw dropped since everything I had ever heard about pit bulls was bad. But at this point my heart was already attached. I was worried about what this could do to our future and if she would be safe around my daughter. So I did what any person in my situation would do, I got educated! I bought books, went online, trained her myself and she became not only a pet, but a family member. She was our Diamond Girl!

Diamond seemed like she needed a playmate. It was now 2005. We had moved out of the apartment and into a house on about two acres and thought it was time to add another dog. But it could not be just any dog. I wanted another pit bull. Now I have had dogs in the past, been around a ton growing up but never did I come across such an amazing breed that wanted nothing but to make you happy, a breed that is so loyal and is always by your side.

Just before Christmas my husband and I were ready to look for another puppy. This time my daughter and Diamond went with us. Diamond was a little overwhelmed but she had no real issues. Several eight-week-old puppies were playing and running around the room but there was one who just had to play with Diamond. Anywhere Diamond went, so did this puppy. So again, we felt like we had been picked and not the other way around.

Yes, we took her home and all I could think was if we had not taken her, someone else might use her for breeding or worse. Anyway, her name is Zoey Monster! What a fitting name. She looks like a monster on the outside but is really just this sweet girl who wants to be loved. Now I had two great additions to the family because to us, that is what they are: family.

By 2013, I had a ten year old and an eight year old pit bull and was looking to add a third dog. We went to the shelter but none of the dogs seemed to get along with our girls. As we were leaving, I spotted a litter of puppies. They were half Rottweiler and half pit bull. They were too small for my girls to play with but that did not stop me from holding one of them. I could not put him down.

I then went and filled out all of the paperwork to adopt him. A few weeks later, I got a phone call to see if I was still interested in him. We took the girls back up to the shelter to meet the puppy. But this time, there was another who picked us! He knew he had to win Diamond over first since she was the most dominant so he walked right up to her and submitted.

After winning Diamond's heart he went and won Zoey's as well. He was about ten weeks old and his name was Rockstar. I was not thrilled with the name so I decided to call him by a few others I had thought might work, to see which one he liked and responded to. First was Rockstar. When calling him by Rockstar, he barely put his head up in acknowledgement. Second was Diesel, again no real response. Finally, I tried Natas. He looked right at me, so I said it again. He started wagging his tail and getting excited. I knew from that moment on his name was Natas. Now I have a Diamond Girl, a Zoey Monster, and a Natas. I spend a great deal of time training all of them and they love us.

I feel like I did not rescue Natas – he rescued me! I have a very rare disease called Ehlers Danlos Syndrome Type lll. It causes me a lot of pain in my joints and muscles. If I do not move around I will hurt more. Natas keeps me moving, he keeps me on my toes. He is my best friend! I wanted to get him trained as a service dog for myself but I could not afford to. Still, even if he cannot be my service dog, he will always be my best friend.

My older dogs play with him, love him and protect him. At first I was afraid of this breed because I was uneducated about the breed, but from now on it will only be pit bulls for me. Pit bulls love you with everything they have. They want nothing more than a belly rub and love in return. They sleep with me, go on vacations with me. I could not imagine my life without them. What I do know is that you should never judge a book by its cover. If you do not read it first, you will never know what it is really all about!

LUNA AND ENZO

THANKS TO TONI WARREN

Enzo

Our pit bull love is not due to one, tug-on-your-heartstrings story, but many little every day joys that our pits have brought to us.

My husband and I recently adopted our second pit bull. The first was a little girl pup we adopted while we were living in Florida before we were married. Luna was wonderful. She was the sweetest dog I had ever met. I had never had a dog before, so I was on the fence, but seeing that adorable little red nose, sitting so properly and calmly through our whole meeting, I could not walk away. I was mush.

She was our first clearance pup. We bought her for only one hundred dollars from a strange and quite frankly, dirty couple who I did not trust, but I could not let her go back home with them. Of course this meant that we were unable to meet her doggie parents or see what circumstances she came from. When she turned three, we realized she was very sick. After months of testing and thousands of dollars in vet bills, a neurologist narrowed it down to three possibilities; all of which would be difficult to treat, if treatable at all. Through broken hearts we had to let her go.

We knew that Luna was perfection as far as a first dog went, especially a first pit. My parents and their friends were literally disgusted when we adopted a pit bull, until they met her. They all cried when they heard the bad news. She did her job of converting so many people into avid pit bull supporters. She was wonderful with their kids and won everyone over so easily. We knew we would always be a pit bull family, from then on.

Our second pit is named Enzo. Only a few months after we lost Luna, my husband surprised me with clearance puppy number two. Seeing that six pound, wrinkly, gray puppy trip and stumble out of the bathroom, wrapped in a big ribbon, I was overwhelmed. My mom, sister and I snuggled with him, but in a few minutes I burst into tears. I had my heart set on rescuing a dog from a shelter. My wonderful husband hugged me and told me we did rescue him. He was from a backyard breeder who almost did not give him up because his friend had already claimed him as a fighting dog.

My heart breaks just writing this. It brings me to tears because I cannot fathom this sweet, fun-loving and snuggly little guy being forced into that life. Though his initial gremlin noises were a little irritating, we quickly learned that like some dogs, he was just vocal when playing. My husband worked hard to teach him good manners and took him for frequent visits to the dog park for socialization.

Enzo and I had a rough first few months. He was the opposite of Luna (I blamed the quarter of Lab in him), chewing everything, tearing everything up, and constantly peeing inside the house. My husband was terribly sick the first two weeks, so I was elected for the middle of the night outdoor trips. This routine was exceptionally miserable because our loft apartment was on the second floor and it was the middle of winter in Rhode Island.

Every time he needed to go out, I had to bundle up in boots, hat, scarf and gloves and force a little puppy sweater on him, praying he would not relieve himself in the meantime. This was only my second puppy and although we were told he was eight weeks old, based on his size and suckling, we think he was younger. I had a hard time training him and may have created a few bad habits, like allowing him to sit on my feet while I made dinner and cleaned the kitchen. My logic was: if I could see him, it meant he was not getting into trouble!

When he was four months old, we went on a quick vacation and I almost cried leaving him with a wonderful family to watch him. It was then I realized how attached to him I had become.

A short time later, he had his first trip to a farm. My friend lives on a small organic farm in central Massachusetts with sheep guarded by a llama. Yes, a llama! Natural enemies of the dog, their llamas have always been more successful than their guard dogs had been at protecting the sheep.

Now we live in Southwestern Virginia. There are many neighboring farms with sheep, horses and goats that Enzo loves to visit. Silly farm dog!

I want to backtrack for a quick story. We got Enzo on December 17, and for Christmas we went to my family's house in Connecticut. My mom did not tell any of the family friends (who so loved Luna) that we got a new puppy because she wanted it to be surprise. That it was! One of the biggest pit bull skeptics, (previously, that is) was standing by the door when we came in. Enzo (just a little six pound gray peanut) came puppy-running in and right to her. She cried out in surprise, picked him up, and slid to the ground in tears holding and loving him.

Even she was taken aback by her own reaction—she said it was just an overwhelming mix of emotions; sadness being reminded of Luna, and the joy of holding this tiny bundle of new pit bull joy in her arms. She was so happy that we rescued another one.

Now that we are in Virginia, with my husband's family and our two-year-old niece, she and Enzo are the best of friends. They have the same curious spirit and he follows her everywhere. One day my mother-in-law was babysitting them both, and Enzo was sniffing around my niece Payton's toy box. She picked up the toy nearest him and babbled to him about it.

Enzo tilted his head, listening intently. She put the toy back, and he nosed at another one, which she picked up and told him about as well. This went on for a while until Enzo was satisfied that he knew all there was to know, and Payton was happy to have taught him. My mother-in-law said it was the cutest thing she had ever seen and still regrets not having it on video.

Enzo also took a liking to Payton's sand box. One hot day he climbed in and was relaxing when Payton wanted to get in and play. She was happy to have a buddy and climbed in right next to him. Enzo did not even flinch as she poured sand all over him and shoved him over as best she could to make room for herself. I truly see why they used to be referred to as Nanny Dogs! Payton's mom loves posting pictures on Facebook of them together as proof that there is no need to be concerned!

Even though I was slow to warm up to Enzo, I am now illogically attached to him for that same reason. He is so full of curiosity, love, and happiness. He makes everyone around him laugh.

His happiness is so contagious that I call him my therapy dog. I have depression and anxiety (usually very subdued, but through the huge changes we have had the past few years of our lives, it tends to sneak out). Just spending the day with Enzo makes me happy. He grabs a toy to show me when he greets me at the door, and shows so much love for life, I cannot help but smile and love life too. I enjoy every day with him and lucky for me, I work from home!

Our dream is to settle down on a large piece of property and start our own pit bull rescue. In every pit bull you meet, you can see the forgiveness and the appreciation for your help and attention. They deserve a chance, and seem to be so grateful when they get one. It is my hope that people will eventually learn that their bad reputations are not the dogs' fault.

DELILAH

THANKS TO KAREN SCHIFFMAN

I was never someone who thought about adopting a pit bull. The reputation was enough for me, but I had recently lost a beloved cat with a huge personality to leukemia. I was devastated and, after some significant mourning, I felt like I needed to bring some new energy into the house.

Since I had two other cats at the time, who were testing negative for the disease, yet had been exposed to my other cat, I did not feel like I could adopt another cat in good conscience. At the same time, an acquaintance in town was trying to arrange a home or at least a foster home for an older dog being fostered by her friends.

This dog was described as very sweet and well behaved. I agreed to let them bring the dog over so I could meet her, but when I was told she was a pit bull, images of an aggressive, unpredictable dog came to mind and I really began to have doubts. I was most concerned for the cats. One was especially affected by my deceased cat's condition. She had begun to urinate in the house and was acting strangely overall.

The day came and I met the dog. Her name was Delilah and what a sweetheart she was with big brown, kind eyes and a beautiful brindle coat. She was very shy and sweet and was just turning eight years old. Her previous owner of seven years decided to move to an apartment where dogs were not allowed, according to the foster family. Because her sweetness was so evident, I immediately agreed to let her stay.

I noticed immediately how comfortable the cats seemed with her also. I had not been sure about leaving them with a dog of any breed while away at work, but I gauged the situation and her temperament and felt that they would be fine. Delilah seemed to help the cat that was having trouble healing. All of her strange behaviors stopped almost immediately and she seemed like herself again. Delilah has helped me more than I can say and has been the best dog I have ever had.

I hope more people look beyond the stigma and open their homes and hearts to these dogs. Delilah has been with me for three years now and I am grateful every day.

MILLIE

THANKS TO KATIE

I have always loved dogs and always wanted to adopt a shelter dog. I was once an addict and have been clean for two years. I am grateful to have a second chance at life. So right before my birthday my boyfriend and I decided to adopt a dog. It would be my birthday gift to myself.

We went to the shelter and fell in love with a couple of dogs but we also have another dog and some cats. After meeting the dogs, we decided they would be too much for our current dog, so the shelter staff started to bring out other dogs that they felt would be a better fit for our family. Finally, they brought out a scared little pittie who looked over-bred, had lost her fur and was way too thin.

Truthfully, I was disappointed. She was not the dog I really wanted but we decided to take her home anyway. I did feel guilty for not being completely in love with her but we had already agreed to take her. Immediately, the woman who had worked with her for the three months she had been there started to cry. She gave me her number and asked me to stay in contact in case I had any questions about our new dog Millie.

Once we brought her home she completely won our hearts. She is now my world. I suffer from depression and when I am sad she always cheers me up. She recently started school to become a therapy dog and the teacher thinks she will do great things.

Millie and I have a bond I will never fully understand but we were both given a second chance. She and I hope to pay it forward as not every human or animal is lucky enough to get a second chance. I love Millie more than life itself. She has changed my life. We are excited for Millie to start her journey toward becoming a therapy dog. We plan to show the world that pitties are amazing dogs. All they need is a chance.

It is hard to imagine what Millie went through in the five years before we found each other, but I am guessing it was not good. So I try to give her the best life possible and give her lots of love. No dog deserves it more than Millie.

WALTER

THANKS TO MARCI BALONICK

My husband and I wanted a dog. We wanted to get a dog from a shelter, but my husband was opposed to getting a pit bull initially. We planned to start a family and were nervous about having a pit bull around children. We went to shelters every week but could not find a dog because the majority of the dogs at the shelters were pit bulls and pit bull mixes.

On January 23, 2011, our neighbors who knew we were looking for a dog told us that their niece, who was in college in Kansas, knew someone that had abandoned a pit bull and her babies at a fraternity party. Their niece took one of the puppies. After discovering that she could not have him in her dorm, brought him home to Chicago for her mom. Her mom was not interested in having a dog, and planned to take the puppy to the shelter. Our neighbors said they knew that we did not want a pit bull but asked if they could bring the puppy over so we could see him before they brought him to the shelter. We said yes, even though we "knew" we were not going to keep him.

Our minds were changed the moment this pit bull puppy stepped into our house. He was the sweetest, cutest, spunkiest puppy and my husband and I instantly fell in love. We told our neighbors that we really liked him but we would have to think about it since we were still hesitant about having a pit bull. Our neighbors offered to keep him for the day before taking him to the shelter in case we changed our minds. It did not take long. Thirty minutes later I went and got the puppy. I told our neighbors we would keep him for the day until we made up our minds.

Here we are three years later and Walter is part of the family. We now have a sixteen month old daughter, Eve. I have had dogs my entire life and Walter is by far the most gentle, well-tempered, sweetest, most tolerant dog I have ever known. Our daughter pulls his hair, sits on him, grabs his toys while he is chewing on them, and he ignores her. He is protective of all of us. If one of us is sick with a cold, he will lay in bed with us. When Eve is crying in her crib Walter sits outside of her room, and will pace the hallways back and forth until we can appease her.

Walter is a riot and extremely smart! He will often pretend he is sleeping, and when my husband or I will get up from the couch he will steal our spot because it has been warmed up for him. He likes to sleep with his head on a pillow and will stand and wait until we get his pillow. He basically housetrained himself and he learns tricks within minutes.

I could go on and on about what a wonderful dog Walter is. My husband and I have been converted – we are pit pull lovers! We were once just like so many others with fears about pit bulls being mean and vicious. Now we know it is the owner and not the breed. We have a few other friends with pit bulls and they are just as sweet as Walter. We would get another pit bull without question!

KENNA, ROSIE, DIESEL AND MAXIMUS

THANKS TO LAUREN LEE

Our family happened by accident. Well, not entirely. I guess I just never envisioned it growing this large. It was going to be just me and my husband, or so was the plan some twelve years ago when we were planning our wedding and building our house. It would be quiet. I would be able to write with no interruptions. We could travel whenever we had the time - and that is how we began.

Two or three years into our happy, new life I suggested to my husband that, since we already agreed we did not want children, we should consider adding the one thing that makes every happy family complete: a dog. We visited a local Animal Welfare organization where we were introduced to several dogs and puppies to see which one we best clicked with.

As it turned out, the decision was not ours to make. Out in the introduction yard, my husband met a beautiful, reddish-brown, medium-sized dog, who had brown, human-looking eyes and ears that stood halfway up and then flopped over. She rolled over, inviting him to rub her belly. It was clear, she had chosen us. We named her Kenna.

Interestingly, all of the adoption paperwork stated that our new dog was a Lab/Golden Retriever mix. I had not been concerned much about the breed, but found it odd that she neither had physical characteristics of a Lab nor did she retrieve anything.

"What breed do you think she is?" I asked at my vet's office, a few days later. Three sets of eyes at the front desk looked at Kenna, back at me, back at Kenna, and returned to me.

"Oh, pit."

"She's definitely got pit bull in her."

"For sure, she's part pit."

I had heard of the pit bull, but nothing specific came to mind.

"Don't worry, pit bulls can make wonderful pets," one of the veterinarians said. I was not worried. Rather, I had not been prior to the moment my trusted veterinarian set up my new dog's file which read "LEE, KENNA" on the tab and had, in large, handwritten letters across the front "P I T B U L L !" I left with a sinking feeling. How could I screw up adopting a dog? And how had I missed some crucial information that apparently everyone else had?

I broke the news to my husband that evening, when he inquired about the vet appointment. "They said they think she is part pit bull," I told him. "So? How old does he think she is? Is she healthy? How was she in the car?"

I thought for a moment. She was fine. No, actually, she was great. She seemed to enjoy riding in the car, though it appeared she preferred the driver's seat. She wagged her tail whenever someone new entered the doctor's office. She definitely showed a fondness for children and was extra gentle, seemingly aware of her size relative to theirs. I decided to trust my instinct. Our family now included a loving, beautiful dog, regardless of breed.

Still, being an avid reader and an educator, the feeling that I had missed a well-circulated memo never sat well with me, so I took it upon myself to do some research. Google™ "pit bull" and one will find as many different definitions as there are dogs on the planet. As far as accuracy and reliability, that is a whole different story. The one thing I can say for sure is that to know a pit bull is to fall in love.

Over the now ten plus years since bringing Kenna home, I have been faced with numerous reactions. Whenever I have mentioned owning a pit some respond positively, others not so well and a few have been downright rude. Kenna has accompanied us to Maine, run along the beach, traveled to numerous ski areas, and brought smiles to the faces of elderly people during visits to a nursing home.

I taught her to sit, lie down, stay, come, speak, give paw, give other paw, give hug, give a high-five, and lift each paw individually for towel drying when she comes in from the rain. She has guarded us, our home, property, the neighbors' homes and the neighbors' children. Everyone who has met Kenna adores her. She is truly in every way, a good dog. Though I did the lion's share of her training, she bonded most with my husband and if it were up to her, she would never leave his side. He knew when he first saw her at the animal shelter. She picked him that day and she is truly man's best friend.

And then there was Rosie. Rosie was a fifty pound white and tan pit bull with a ring around one eye that resembled the RCA dog or Petey from "The Little Rascals." I heard of Rosie from a friend of mine who was fostering her while living in Florida. When my friend got a job in Connecticut she left Rosie in Florida with her mom who was retired and already had one dog of her own and was a foster for another one. She did not want a third. Next thing

I knew, I was driving from Connecticut to Florida and back again, over one Thanksgiving weekend, to pick up Rosie. And then there were two.

There were some adjustment issues to work out. Who liked what toys, which dog got possessive over toys, whether or not there would be issues surrounding food, walking two dogs together. Kenna was clearly in charge of the house, but Rosie would always be right behind her. Kenna was serious. Rosie was playful and quirky. Kenna was always doing a job. She stood guard, helping with projects in the yard, sitting in the window watching the road for non-residents, seemingly like an occupation. Rosie was a free spirit, often wandering off the property or howling at the night sky. She would amuse herself endlessly tossing her red ball up in the air and kicking it around.

I must admit I felt a special love for Rose. She came with scars that spoke of a rough start in life. Looking closely, it was apparent that another dog had bitten parts of her big, floppy ears. The records from the rescue organization indicated that when they found her, she was living on the street, barely skin and bones. Rosie's exact age was unclear. What was clear was that she had never had a loving home where she was safe. There was no indication she had any formal training, as she pulled on a leash. She chased every wild animal she could find.

As agile and strong as she was, the poor girl could never walk from point A to point B in a straight line. Rather, she became confused. If anything was in her path that required her to navigate, walking around or stepping over, she just did not have that ability. She did not even know to walk off the driveway to a grassy spot to do her business. My husband would occasionally refer to her as "stupid" or "special," which I pleaded with him not to do within earshot of

Rosie, somehow convinced that hearing this would further damage this sweet girl.

Kenna seemed to think she was human, no different from me and my husband. If she wore a sign, it would read, "Chief Proprietor of the Lee Estate." Rosie's would read, "Doesn't Play Well with Others." As with many abused dogs, Rosie never learned how to play and despite her best efforts to make friends with other dogs, her behavior came across as too rough or threatening. Suffice it to say, she would not be an optimal candidate for dog parks and playdates. So, I went out of my way to play with her, love her, hang out with her. I promised her I would make up for all she lacked in her early years.

Despite her quirks, Rosie has a sweet and gentle heart and a keen ability to key into human emotion. When I am sick or sad, the first to be lying on top of me is Rosie, who will often gently place her face against mine. Over time she began to lift her paw to our cheeks and "pet" us, as she has seen us do to her with our hands. In Rosie's mind, the great outdoors is a giant hunting ground, likely a survival skill picked up in her early life. This survival skill cost us approximately seven thousand dollars in fencing for the front and back of our property.

"That is one expensive rescue dog," my husband has said. If that is the only seven grand I unexpectedly have to spend in my lifetime, I figure I am lucky. Every day, within that fenced property, I can find someone who loves me more than anyone in the world. It is a little dog with a brown spot around one eye, her tail wagging, often carrying her favorite red ball in tow. Her name is Rosie and she is my best friend.

Our family had become a happy foursome. It was pretty clear we would always be a pittie family. I spent a few summers volunteering at the local Animal Shelter, where I trained some of the dogs that might be considered more difficult. My husband only had one stipulation: Do not bring any more dogs home. After vet bills, fence bills, dog food, and the cost and arrangement of dog care when we traveled, our lives had become significantly more complicated than they started out.

One of my summer charges was Hopkins, a medium-sized, muscular, white and brindle pit bull who came into the shelter with the name Diesel. That was changed in the interest of a less aggressive, more "adoption friendly" name. He had ended up at the shelter after repeatedly being picked up by the local animal control officer. Apparently, his owner did not care enough to keep him inside and out of harm's way. The smart little guy returned each night though, to the safety of a neighbor's lawn furniture where he curled up and waited for the animal control officer. He was an affectionate and energetic guy. I figured Hopkins would be an easy boy to train.

Then I was told the four words that I would later hear so many times when prospective adopters would walk through the shelter and admire Hopkins, "But he is deaf." This would be a challenge but for me, failure was not an option. I grabbed a leash, filled my pockets with treats, took Hopkins outside to a grassy area, and with a certain sense of urgency, I decided to prove this dog had ability.

It was not the immediate success I had imagined. After a couple of days I realized that in the dog world, butterflies, shadows, and passing cars rank high among the top most interesting things, and I was not on that short list.

Then I looked at things from another perspective. What if the issue was not the lack of hearing, but rather a lack of trust? After all, from the limited knowledge I had, this guy was born without the ability to hear. What he never had was a relationship with a human who loved him enough to give him a sense of security. I walked him to a shady area where we could sit together and I made the shape of the letter "D" (for Diesel) with the fingers on my right hand. I did this several times. I would tap him, show him the "D," and get his attention. It would be our little secret that I had changed his name back to Diesel, but I felt it fit him better. He did not seem to disagree.

From there we progressed to "Diesel, sit." I would tap him, make the sign for "D" then hold my hand up leaning toward him, making the hand motion for sit. It turned out this dog was one smart little man. In less than two months, he learned "sit," "lie down," "come," "stay," "no" and a few signs I threw in for fun, such as "play roughhouse." It was like a whole world of communication had been unlocked for him.

As the weeks went on and "Hopkins," as I had address him inside the shelter, came to expect my regular visits and training sessions, he began to bark nonstop when he saw me enter the kennel area. If I could translate dog, I would imagine he was saying, "Finally! Take me out now! Let the fun begin! I worried you would not be back for me. Let's go!"

I went back nearly every day that summer. It became about more than the enjoyment I got out of volunteering or the challenge of training dogs. I fell in love with that little guy with the white floppy ears, who spent the majority of his days in a kennel, waiting for our time together.

Unfortunately, the staff at the shelter did not translate Diesel's barking into the enthusiastic words I did. Instead, they saw a barking pit bull as a deterrent to potential adopters and moved him from a prominent front kennel to a kennel in the very back of the dog room. My heart sank each day when we would come in and he would automatically go to his usual kennel, until I redirected him to the rear of the building.

"You have to think of how it looks," a young volunteer said to me. "A lot of people are afraid of pit bulls." Several people who saw me working with Diesel inquired about him or remarked what a cute dog he was. "But he is deaf," another volunteer or employee usually added.

"But he is trained to respond to hand signals," I tried to say, but by the time I got the words out, the person or persons had moved on. Diesel did not know he was any different from other dogs. He was unaware that other dogs could hear and he could not. He had no idea that people were afraid of him because of his body type. He had no knowledge of the "bad rap" associated with dogs of his breed and the controversy often surrounding the pit bull breeds.

I suppose he was, like so many people, a victim of human prejudice and ignorance. Diesel only knew that as people walked through the kennel area, he was not the one chosen to walk to the front desk. Or stand with a human as he or she filled out the paper work, and then go outside to the human's car, where he would be driven off to live happily ever after.

Despite my husband's words still clear in my mind, I held out hope that little Diesel might tug at his heart strings too. Despite his lack of expressiveness, my husband is an animal lover who would never turn away an animal in need. Granted, training, cleaning and disciplining animals falls on me, but when it comes down to it, he would take in every needy animal if he could.

I was painfully aware that the summer was drawing to a close, I would be returning to teaching full-time, and the thought of Diesel left in a kennel, feeling abandoned again made me sadder than I could say. He and I had developed a close bond. We both taught one another how to communicate that summer. I begged my husband to come and meet him.

And so it happened that my husband and I struck a balance between "Don't bring anymore dogs home" and "Let's take this one!" I agreed to foster Diesel. I set up my extra dog crate and bed at home in a big room beside Kenna's and Rosie's crates. I prepared food and water dishes, and bought Diesel his own bed for inside his crate, and on an unusually hot late August day, I went to the shelter to take Diesel home with me. As usual, he was excited to see me, but, he knew something was different. I truly think he knew this was his day because he pulled me through the doors, outside, and – not to our regular training yard or walking route—but to my car, which he jumped into before I could fully open the back door. He would be Diesel from now on and he would be mine.

Anyone who has rescued a pet has seen the look of sincere appreciation – the way an animal says "thank you" with his or her whole body. Thank you for saving my life. Thank you for giving me a place to sleep. It does not matter how much or how little you give because it is far more than that animal ever had before you. That was Diesel. While some dogs have crate anxiety, he jumped into his own crate and cherished it. It did not make a bit of difference that his was slightly smaller than the other dogs'. He was an easy fit in our family. The other dogs were aware that something was different about him, but they quickly made it their responsibility to look after their new little brother.

Kenna taught him how to guard: front paws on the windowsill, fiercely barking, in the event that someone who did not actually own property on our road might travel through. Diesel, a quick student, not only began guarding, but began to sense when cars turned down our road and would jump from the sofa across the room to the window, sounding fierce as could be.

But for all his fierce sounding bravado, Diesel is a true pit bull. His attacks came in the form of big, wet kisses. He enjoys running around the fenced in yard, but enjoys it most when our friends next door come over. Mollie is five and Jack is three and they too have developed a special bond with Diesel. It is clear why pit bulls were originally titled "The Nanny Dog," known for their love of and ability to look after children. Often, Diesel can be found in the front yard, by the edge of the fence that faces Mollie and Jack's house, hoping they will come out to play. Mollie has learned to use hand signals with Diesel, communicating with him in a way he understands.

I suppose you could say Diesel was my "foster failure." He was actually my biggest success. I helped him to communicate, and opened up a world for him that had previously been overlooked by humans. Whatever I gave to him, he has given back to our family tenfold. I guess I did not really want to foster him. Fostering would mean eventually giving him up and I could never do that, even to the best of homes. Little Diesel is my heart.

Recently, my husband and I adopted a fourth pit bull. I found Maxi on a rescue organization's Facebook feed. Of course, when a home could not be found for this man, we stepped up. We are still getting to know our new puppy. At one year old and eight-five pounds, he finds everything fascinating. He loves to test the limits, chews what he can find—especially if it is valuable to us, and wraps one paw around both legs if I try to walk away from a game of play. He makes us laugh daily. Maxi will be another story altogether. I am thinking he might even be a book.

Our family did not exactly happen by accident. It happened with a lot of love. Every furry addition has added so much joy, so many smiles, and lots of laughter. I laugh when I think back upon my initial visit to the vet with Kenna, our first rescue. I chuckle at my own ignorance and anxiety upon hearing, "pit bulls can make very good pets."

Yes they can. I cannot imagine life without a pit bull.

PART FIVE

RESCUES

I waited very patiently, the days they came and went

Today's the day I thought, my family will be sent.

Then just when I began to think it wasn't meant to be,

There were people standing there just gazing down at me.

I knew them in a heartbeat, I could tell they felt it too.

They said, "We have been waiting for a special dog like you."

Now every night I say a prayer to all the gods that be,

"Thank you for the life I live and all you've given me.

But most of all protect the dogs in the pound and on the street

And send a rescue person to lift them off their feet."

Excerpt from "Once I Was a Lonely Dog"

~Arlene Pace (September 18, 1998)

CARLIE MASHED POTATOES

THANKS TO KATHIE WEINBERG –
HOME SWEET HOME RESCUE

Back in early November 2012, New Jersey had just been struck by Hurricane Sandy. I received a call on Sunday, November 11 from a rescue group trying to place a stray pocket pit bull from Philadelphia who was scheduled to be euthanized on that day at 6:00 p.m. Did I know anyone? Could I help find a foster?

The only experience that I had with pit bulls was driving a transport of five up to Massachusetts a few weeks before. All my personal dogs are small poodle types and I had only fostered other small dogs.

The search for someone to take her was futile, so I agreed. I thought I could crate her in an extra bedroom, separate from the other dogs in case she was aggressive toward them. I did not know what she would be like and I was pretty scared.

Carlie was transported to my house by a wonderful volunteer. She was tiny, maybe 25 pounds and very quiet. She greeted me with a kiss. She met my dogs outside and could not have been friendlier.

She wrapped herself up in the blankets on my bed and must have slept for two days - she was tired.

Carlie was also cold. I think that she must have been cold her whole life as her second favorite place was laying as close as she could to the wood-burning stove for hours on end. He favorite spot was wrapped up in a blanket with me on the couch.

My daughter visited at Christmas and nicknamed her Mashed Potatoes because she was so mushy, creamy and felt so good.

I realized on Christmas Eve last year that Mashed Potatoes would not be going anywhere, that she had found her forever home and I officially adopted her.

So as the months passed, I continued to foster other small dogs, but was most excited when I brought home bigger playful puppies. As I drove them to my home, I felt like I was bringing Mashed Potatoes a Christmas present. I would giggle with delight as I watched Carlie do back flips of excitement at the sight of a new friend.

I should mention that she was also the "Belle of the Ball" at her doggy daycare. All the other dogs loved her and she them.

I remember in April of 2013, how excited I was bringing home Charlie, a six month old Wheaton puppy. I was at the shelter, and said "I will take him." Another present for Carlie!

I happened to be short on bedding, so I took a homemade dog bed with me for Charlie. Within the next few days, my Mashed Potatoes chewed up Charlie's bedding. Little did I know that it had been made of some sort of older, low quality stuffing! This stuffing actually looked like fishing wire and it became lodged in her intestines.

On April 24, 2013 she died in my arms as a result of the surgery to remove the blockage. Even though I had seven other dogs at home, the house felt empty without her. I buried her in my backyard and made a garden on the site.

I cry as I write this. Carlie Mashed Potatoes was such a wonderful dog, friend and companion. She was a true ambassador for the breed and forever changed my view of pit bulls. https://www.facebook.com/homesweethomeanimalrescueinc

TEACHING THEM TO BE "JUST DOGS"

THANKS TO DANIELLE SALINO – MARLEY'S ANGELS

Over the past three years I have fostered dozens of pit bulls from the New York Animal Care and Control and have adopted five. Two of the five are unadoptable and were going to be put to sleep. I felt I could not let that happen so I kept them. I currently have thirteen shelter dogs. Six are mine, three are fosters, two are sanctuaried, and one is in hospice. I shelter, feed, train, and provide medical care for all of them.

We have in our care throwaway moms, dogs abandoned in a family home for months after the family moved, physically abused dogs, neglected dogs, etc. We teach them to trust, return dignity to them, nurse them back to health physically and emotionally, and teach them all they need to know to just be dogs. Some did not even know how to play, let alone basic manners. Socialization is almost always needed. Some have fear aggression while others are just afraid – of crates, men, women, hats, brooms, hoses, etc.

My love for dogs has put me on this path to help the helpless and to be a voice for the voiceless. Anything I can do to help them get the recognition they deserve is why I am here.

Oh, I forgot to mention which were the pit bulls, all but three. I currently have nine—three females and six males. All are awesome dogs in their own right. All have overcome their issues to be great loving, obedient, loyal, friendly dogs.

Pit bull was not the breed we chose but the breed that chose us-we are the lucky ones. https://www.facebook.com/HappyPicklePants?fref=ts

VINCENZO
STILL CHANGING LIVES

THANKS TO ANGELA LAFRANCE – ePITome DOG RESCUE

I have many stories, but the one that means the most to me is the story of our Vincenzo. He was our very first pit bull.

I was scared to death to bring him into my house, but I did it for my son. As it turns out this was one of the best decisions of my life. Vinny taught me so much about pit bulls. He was one of the strongest influences in my life, ever.

Vinny was and always will be my heart dog. We lost him at only four years old to Lymphoma. A little over a year after Vin passed away, I started ePITome Dog Rescue. After the hurt of losing Vinny, I told my daughter that I would never have another pit bull in my home because there could only be one Vinny. She asked, "But, Mom, what was the point of Vinny being in your life if you are not going help other pit bulls?" ePITome is his legacy.

I feel so blessed to be able to rescue, and to know that the dogs that we save go on to be amazing, life changing, and positive influences in the lives of others.

I can never fully explain the impact Vin had on me, but I am a different person now than before he entered my life. I would like to think I am a better person for having been loved by him and getting the honor of being his mama. I wanted to share our story because I want the world to know about a wonderful pit bull named Vincenzo who is still changing lives from beyond this life. https://www.facebook.com/epitomedogrescue

GULLIVER

THANKS TO JEANIE CHRISTENBURY – INDEPENDENT RESCUER

I am an independent rescuer and I live in Mint Hill, North Carolina. Almost two years ago, a family that had adopted a dog from me called on a Sunday night to see if I could take a young dog they found running in the road in upstate South Carolina. I agreed and my friend Connie and I drove to meet her.

When I saw the dog, my heart dropped because I saw he was mostly a pit bull and I knew his chances of being adopted would be slim. I already had three dogs, one of which had been attacked two years earlier by another dog, an attack that almost killed her. She was no longer the congenial dog she had been and did not like any new dogs coming to the house.

So began my fostering of a boy named Gulliver. My friend Connie helped me a lot in the beginning, working with him on his training. He was a good dog but nothing special it seemed. I advertised in newspapers, with local pit bull rescues, and by word-of-mouth to everyone I met that either had a pit bull or that I knew would be open to adopting one.

Now, almost two years later, with no interest at all from my ads to get him a home, he has become mine. Gulliver sleeps with me at night and he adores my young grandchildren. I recently rescued a kitten and he is fascinated and wants to play with her but has not tried to harm her. I would never have believed I would own a pit-tie, much less allow him to sleep in the bed with me and my other dogs.

DAGNY THE INCREDIBULL

THANKS TO RAFI JOHNSON – WILLY'S HAPPY ENDINGS and SEAN CASEY ANIMAL RESCUE

I am the Director of Willy's Happy Endings (W.H.E.), a senior and special needs dog rescue located in Tennessee. We focus on the hardest to place and most costly demographic of dogs in shelters and we love our work.

I, personally, have a passion for pit bull-type dogs as well. So naturally, we rescue as many of them as we are able.

Several months ago, the board and I decided that it would be wonderful to find a spokes dog for our rescue. A young dog with special needs to train for therapy work, etc. and show that special needs dogs are capable of being vibrant, brilliant, unflinchingly loyal family pets and more – and also to encourage the adoption of special needs dogs. I also asked that we find a pit bull-type dog in order to advocate for bully breeds in addition to 'specials' (as we call them here at W.H.E.).

Over the course of about six months, I temperament tested a few dogs locally, but none fit the bill. One day, a photo came to my attention—a little white pit bull with a crooked pink face. Her name was Angel, and I loved her immediately.

Angel was found near death in a New York City park as a puppy after having suffered a traumatic attack. Animal control officers suspected she had been used as a bait dog. Her skull and jaw had been crushed and she had multiple deep punctures all over. Luckily, the people of Sean Casey Animal Rescue (SCAR) saw her at the shelter and pulled her into the safety of their program. She underwent multiple surgeries to repair her shattered jaw and remove bone fragments that were causing severe infection. There was irreparable damage to her facial structure, which left her with a sagging eye, a crooked jaw, and temporomandibular joint and muscle disorders (also known as TMJ). Once she recovered, it became obvious that she was also completely deaf.

Due to her unique looks, and disability, no one wanted to adopt the little deformed puppy. She sat in a kennel, well loved by the staff and rescue volunteers, but without a home of her own for eight months. During this time, she met Christine and Sofie, a stellar mother-daughter duo doing amazing things for the homeless dogs of New York City through a Facebook page (NYC Teens for

Animals). Sofie worked with Angel all summer long, and shared her photo on the Facebook page.

I contacted SCAR and Christine and Sofie to let them know I was interested. They sent me videos and pictures showing her vast potential and wonderful temperament. About a week later, she was on her way to us in Tennessee.

I gave her a new name, Dagny, which means new day in Old Norse, and loved her more than I could describe. The connection was immediate. I felt as though there had been something missing in my life before she came and I did not even know it. She arrived at our hectic house filled with eight other dogs, cats, and three young children, and just settled in with us like she had always been here.

Dagny has a zest and appreciation for life unmatched by any dog I have ever met. Every new thing she experiences is a gift to her. She soaks it all in with a classic pittie smile and learns so fast. She has begun formal training to become a therapy dog for hospitalized children and is learning faster than many dogs without disabilities.

Dagny is learning through positive reinforcement with hand signals and excelling at every new command and behavior. One day soon she will be visiting children who have had traumatic accidents and illnesses and offering strength and hope to them in their time of need. She will also attend events and fundraisers as an advocate for bully breeds and special needs dogs!

She is a complete cuddle bug and an absolute clown, giving us more smiles than I can count and endless laughter and companionship.

She has overcome so much and yet remains an amazing creature who is literally always smiling. We humans could take a lesson from her in forgiveness and positivity. I am so grateful to have her in my life.

She is a true example of the resilience, loyalty, and gentle nature of pit bull type dogs and is going to make a difference in the world! https://www.facebook.com/DagnyTheIncredibull

DUCHESS

THANKS TO REBECCA MORLEY – REBECCA'S ANIMAL RESCUE ENTERPRISES

I am a 43-year-old transplanted Australian, living and working in TV commercial production in Los Angeles. I had dogs growing up my entire life (German Shepard, Black Lab, and English Bull Dog). I adopted my pit bull two years ago and I never expected what ended up happening to happen.

I found her online on the Pet Pardons website. Her intake photo was sad and the description was worse. It was her eyes that got me. They pleaded with me even through the computer. I could not imagine what it was like to meet her in person. I took off immediately to the shelter, not thinking for a second of the consequences.

What could be different with a pit bull? I could never have imagined what happened next. Her body was riddled with scars, cuts, puncture wounds and her weight was so low you could see every bone in her body. As I prepared to bring her home, I prepared myself for the worst.

My fears were unfounded. She was a sweetheart from the first moment I saw her, wanting only love and affection. She slept with me in my bed. She never left my side. She never barked or made a single sound. No one could tell me why she would not bark. She just chose to be silent. So silent that my roommate and the land-lady, unless I told them, had no idea I even had a dog at all. After revealing this however, we were both thrown out, as the house I rented was pet friendly, just not pit bull friendly.

I embarked on the most prejudiced search for housing I had ever known. I never imagined that the problems I was going to encounter with a pit bull had nothing to do with the dog itself but with peoples' perception of them and their frenzy of fear and ill-informed hysteria, causing property managers and landlords to flat out reject me for no reason.

It took us three months to find housing. I would drag her along to every open house that said pet friendly. I would call and let them know she is 80 pounds and a bully breed. She is actually an American Bully and has no pit bull in her. I would always make sure I was being upfront and correct about my dog. I only wanted to live in a place where she was welcome.

I finally came across one property manager who got it. He ran my background check. I am a landlord's dream. I have no debt, have been doing my job for the past 23 years, have good credit, a flawless renting history and come with good references. One particular property manager went to bat for me and the landlords wanted me too, however, once again we were tripped up by the homeowners' insurance policy that had it in fine print that the landlords never saw – "your insurance policy will be null and void if any pit bull breed resides on the premises." They asked me to take out a $2,200 annual vicious breed insurance policy, which I agreed to, but the insurance company would not accept it.

I was back out on the streets looking. I almost had to live in my car. I would have done anything for that dog. Eventually I found the place I am living in now. The property manager confessed to owning a pit bull and told me it was the best dog he had ever had. We moved in forty-eight hours later and he did not even ask for an additional pet deposit.

Many ask me, "Why would you go to such lengths for a dog?" I have never had a connection like this with any of my other dogs. There is an indescribable feeling I get when she is by my side and looks directly into my eyes, never making a sound except little whimpers when I rub her belly or kiss her face. I have never experienced a single moment of loneliness since she has come into my life. I will never be able to repay her for that. The world can be such a lonely place.

Shortly after settling into the new place, Duchess was diagnosed with cancer. For the past two years it has been a constant battle of cutting out massive cell tumors that pop up all over her body. I have gone from being debt free with good credit to tens of thousands in credit card debt but I still maintain that I made a promise to her that I would protect her no matter what. I plan on keeping that promise. The sense of well-being I get from making good on my responsibility and promises is better than anything money can buy. I feel like I am capable of achieving anything with her by my side. Many people say, "She is so lucky you rescued her," and my reply is, "she rescued me."

I also run my own pit bull puppy rescue, which was inspired by Duchess. She assists with teaching the puppies how to be dogs. I teach the pups obedience and potty training. Together we rescue the most abused, sick and abandoned puppies, rehabilitate them and then find them good homes. I could not do this rescue without Duchess. All the new adopters ask the same questions, "Why does my male dog pee sitting down?" and "Why is my puppy so quiet?" It would seem that Duchess' traits rubbed off on the puppies. Our latest rescue is a partially paralyzed puppy that was found dumped in a trash can in Compton. Her name is Aurora. The cycle continues. https://www.facebook.com/RebeccasAnimalRescueEnterpris es?fref=ts

SURVIVING AGAINST ALL ODDS - NORMM and OP

THANKS TO ST. LOUIS STRAY RESCUE – RANDY GRIM

NORMM

In the heat of the day during a record-breaking heat wave, Stray Rescue received a Citizen's Service Bureau report about an injured dog—in an area well known for dogfighting.

With no idea what to expect and no knowledge about the severity of the injuries, I rushed to the area. When I arrived, it was like looking for a needle in a haystack. There were abandoned buildings, litter, and overgrown yards everywhere.

I was searching high and low when the resident who reported the abandoned, injured dog waved me down an alley. I scanned a cluttered backyard for any signs of life, and then I saw him –a black, balled-up heap, buried deep within an overgrowth of weeds and under a broken fence.

In temperatures over one hundred degrees, it was clear that this poor dog had crawled there to die. As I got closer, I could smell infection. I saw him take a short shallow breath, and that was enough. I immediately picked up his nearly lifeless body and rushed him to the Stray Rescue Trauma Center, alerting the staff that I was bringing in a dying dog as I drove.

As I drove back to the shelter, I kept telling him to hang in there. That he would know love, safety, and comfort if he could just hang on a little longer. He fought like crazy to live, and we were going to do everything possible to make sure he survived. I named him Normm.

When I arrived, the vet team was waiting. They immediately put his dangerously dehydrated body on fluids and assessed the situation. Normm needed to lose one leg immediately, and we decided to send him for an emergency amputation.

I received word later that day that they were able to successfully amputate the leg, but that was only the first step in Normm's long and uncertain road to recovery.

Now, after weeks of tears, uncertainty, and defying all odds, Normm has made an unbelievable recovery. I picked him up from Veterinary Specialty Services, and the staff said goodbye to this brave boy. I put him in the Jeep, overcome by the now vibrant look in his eyes and the hop in his step, regardless of having a leg amputated.

Welcome to your new life Normm. You are going to love it, and your story will encourage countless people to be caring, responsible, and respectful towards other companion animals.

OP

In late September 2010, we responded to a call about a dog that had been tossed in a dumpster and left to die. He had been shot at least 12 times and strangled by an electrical cord.

The rescued dog, formerly known as Extension but now named OP, short for Optimus Prime, is a striking reminder of both the resiliency of our four-legged friends, as well as the violence of which people are capable.

This dog suffered unspeakable abuse and was knocking on death's door. Thanks to the dedication and compassion of Stray Rescue staff, Veterinary Specialty Services, the Refuse Department, and Animal Care and Control, OP is likely experiencing trust, safety, and comfort for the first time. It is truly miraculous, and his story can motivate people to continue standing up to this unacceptable criminal behavior.

OP, who was paralyzed and lost the use of his back legs walked out of the hospital following his miraculous recovery, with the help of a donated, custom-built cart. OP received intensive medical attention at Veterinary Specialty Services for weeks. This resilient, sweet dog was aided by a cart that was custom built by Stray Rescue supporter and race car driver, Aaron Wood.

With the formation of the Mayor Francis Slay Animal Abuse Task Force, and Stray Rescue of St. Louis dealing with a multitude of cruelty calls, animal abuse and neglect cases have been a widely discussed topic of concern in recent months. The Task Force continues to make a significant difference, averaging an arrest every week. A man has been arrested in connection with this case and is being charged with animal abuse.

The fact that OP's abuser could be brought to justice after this violent crime shows that the Mayor's task force continues to make strides in the fight against animal abuse and neglect in our neighborhoods. The message that this criminal behavior will not be tolerated is getting louder.

I knew in my heart this collaboration making up the task force would work, and it has. These cases are tough, but Stray Rescue does everything we can to save these deserving lives. I am overjoyed to take him home and close this painful chapter of his life. https://www.facebook.com/StrayRescue?fref=ts

KAYLA

THANKS TO JEANIE SCHULZ –
ANIMAL RESCUE KINSHIP (ARK)

As a rescuer, I have many stories, but I can tell you about the one that easily makes the top of my list. Her name is Kayla and she is mine. I had been working in rescue and been a dog trainer for many years before I met Kayla and did not have a whole lot of bully experience. I knew there was misrepresentation, and I was familiar with the Michael Vick case and had just begun researching Breed Specific Legislation and dogfighting issues.

I always liked bully breeds but I had no idea just how much I would come to love them—that is, until Kayla walked into my life. As with everyone in rescue, I was constantly getting animals "dumped" on me for lack of a better term. This was the case with my Kayla. Her owners hit hard times and left Kayla with me and I never heard from them again. She had been moved multiple times and was severely neglected.

From day one since I have had her, she has shown how unique she truly is (and I come across a lot of dogs). The first thing I noticed was her unusual awareness and that she was very intuitive. If ever an animal reached into my soul, I would say she definitely did. She had all kinds of medical and dental problems when I got her and I had no idea how old she was, but I knew she was going to thrive with even the tiniest bit of love thrown her way. You know that moment when you look in their eyes and you can tell that they are survivors and that they want to live? Well that is the look she gave me.

After I had her for a few months, I began working on getting her certified to become a service dog. We were out walking one day and I ran into my friend whose 19 year old daughter had just died of brain cancer. This was her second child to have brain cancer (the first one has been in remission for the last five years). There were no words to describe the pain that this woman was in.

I ended up sitting on a park bench with her and I looked down at Kayla and she was responding so much to all the raw emotion coming from this woman. She kept reaching out to this woman and, next thing you know, they were hugging and kissing. All I could do is watch in amazement as she sat next to my friend and quietly comforted her. I ended up walking my friend home with Kayla in tow. When we got back to her house, I introduced Kayla to my friend's other three children, all elementary age boys. The only way I know to describe the three boys is shell-shocked. They were obviously still reeling from their sister's death. The kids were wise beyond their years and looked like they had been crushed by life. I then watched as Kayla walked over to each kid, including the oldest son that has been in remission, and soothed them.

I am not kidding you when I say this but it was like she had picked out the best way to soothe each one of them and proceeded to care for them accordingly. All on her own, without any coaxing from me, and in her unique pit way. It did not take long before I realized that they needed Kayla way more than I did so Kayla is officially on permanent loan to them. The kids send me cards and pictures all the time and they have told me that Kayla was the best gift they have ever gotten. That she has done more for them than the grief counselors and therapy groups they had gone to. I miss her every day but I know she is right where she should be.

I never get tired of telling people how great these dogs are—the fact that they can come from a dogfighting life or a life of abuse and neglect and then go on to become therapy dogs is a testament of just how great this breed is.

SABLE (BOO BOO BEAR)

THANKS TO FOSTER MOM LAUREN THOMAS AND
SARGE'S ANIMAL RESCUE WAYNESVILLE, NC

I foster for an animal rescue called Sarge's Animal Rescue in Waynesville, North Carolina and have done so for quite some time. I wanted to tell you about Sable the pit bull and her happy story. When Sable came to Sarge's, she was fresh out of the county shelter and it appeared she had recently given birth. She would hoard stuffed animals and react to them like her puppies. It was both adorable and immensely sad.

I decided to foster her when no one else came forward. We simply do not have a lot of pit bull fosters in our organization. She was a wonderful, loving dog who was so funny to watch and play with and just a joy to be around.

It was discovered that she had to have surgery on her knees due to Luxating Patellas. We all pulled together to raise money for the operation.

Then one day, an elderly woman came into Sarge's and said she was looking for a pit bull. Of course we were all surprised, because she looked like she would want a poodle or Chihuahua or terrier, but no, she wanted a pit bull. She said she loved how friendly they were, and then she told us the other reason: her husband was in the late stages of terminal cancer and they both wanted her to have a good loyal dog to protect her if need be. I met her husband and Bonnie (the adopter) and decided it was a good fit. Bonnie adopted Sable in January.

Sarge's recently got a letter from her with an update about Sable:

Sarge's Animal Rescue,

"I don't know if you remember me, probably not, you have so many people wanting pets. My husband was dying when we were there January 5, 2013. You were kind enough to let us adopt Sable. My husband renamed her Boo Boo Bear. My husband passed away on January 31, 2013. Boo has been my lifeline now that I am alone. Be assured Boo gets only the best. She is happy, healthy, playful, and so very loving. I do not have a lot of money but I hope the enclosed check will help. I have also enclosed a picture of Boo my husband took. In the short time my husband had to live she was a comfort to him. He died at home with Boo on one side of him and me on the other."

Gratefully,

Bonnie [last name withheld]

Enclosed with this letter was a check for one thousand dollars.

I loved this dog and I thought about adopting her several times, but I am glad I did not. She had bigger things she needed to accomplish. She touched the lives of everyone at the rescue. You will be hard pressed to find a core volunteer who does not remember that dog. I miss her still to this day but I know I made the right choice. https://www.facebook.com/sarges?fref=ts

LILY, GIGI AND MEATHEAD

THANKS TO JENN HULL

I rescue senior pit bulls. I have had some people ask, "That's a bit risky, isn't it? Nine years of unknown history?" I have adopted three of the "Elderbulls" I have rescued. Lily was a deaf ten year old at the local humane society when I got her. Gigi followed shortly as an eight year old with scars all over her head and face. I could not have asked for two better girls.

Lily yodels and due to arthritis has this adorable swagger. She is the best for cuddling and loves her tennis balls.

Gigi tucks her head between your legs when she wants to be loved, which is pretty much all of the time. She herds my daughter, and is protective of her in a non-aggressive way. One night I snuck up on my daughter to surprise her. As I jumped out she screamed. Gigi being forever the protector, was right there, stepped in between us and herded Addi away from me.

We recently added a seven year old pitty named Meathead to our mix. I saw him on Craigslist being offered for free. We went to visit him at this home in East St. Louis, Missouri and he came home with us the same day. He is underweight with an ear infection but we will have him good as new in no time.

I cannot imagine life without my dogs, and I really cannot believe the need for senior pit bull rescue. So I am starting my own. Hopefully by next year, Mount Ever Rest will be up and running.

WALTER AND RUPERT

THANKS TO DONNA CODYKO – REEERANCH

Walter

Seven years ago I left Connecticut and I bought a small ranch in Kentucky where I could provide a safe place for neglected or at-risk animals, to either live out their lives or be adopted into the right homes. I currently have seven canine residents that are "lifers," meaning they will not or cannot be adopted for various reasons— either due to handicaps or aggression.

About two years ago I was offered an opportunity to go back to Connecticut/New York for my job and be closer to my family for a while. But after a year and a half it was enough and I wanted to get back home to my passion, rescue.

I decided when I went back home to Kentucky, I would take one deserving city dog back with me and give him the amazing and spoiled life that my other dogs enjoy. Yes, we have plenty of dogs in need here. I can pick up a new one every day on the side of the road, and I do. I bring them to other rescues when I am at capacity.

It was at that point I met Walter. In May of 2013, my whole life changed not by the move or the job, but because of a really big dog. I went to the Shelton Dog Pound for two reasons: 1) I knew Sheryl [the Animal Control Officer] and I know what little support she gets to care for the dogs in her care, and 2) it is my hometown.

As I walked from kennel to kennel recognizing that most were pit bulls, I saw the same need amongst all of them—they just wanted to be someone's friend. That being said, I also knew they all needed different care according to individual circumstances. They were not bad but just needed different styles of co-habitation or environment. The first time I went, I saw Walter and thought, "I do not know about this, he looks intimidating, could he be tolerant of all the different dogs I have at my place?" We live like a family. I had dogs from ten pounds to one hundred and ten pounds (from pit mixes to Jack Russell Terriers to hounds) living in peace with each other, sharing a room, sofa and food bowls. As I handed out treats to each of them, Walter sat patiently wagging his tail and took the treat from me like a gentleman. He was sweet and grateful.

I then decided to bring my Jack Russell into the picture as he is the test model/ambassador to the place we call "The ReeeRanch." If Jack accepts you, you get a pass. Jack and Walter hit it off immediately. Although Jack was not entirely happy that Walter shoved his nose up Jack's backside and made a mini wheelbarrow out of him in the pound parking lot! Jack understood though that this enormous goofy dog was just not aware of his own enormous size!

A few days later we were off. It was a sixteen hour drive, split into two eight hour days with a night in a hotel in between. Both dogs displayed stellar behavior. They even shared the second bed in the hotel room where Walter demonstrated his comedic side as well as his very loving and cuddly side. He immediately drew the other hotel guests' attention as we bulldozed through the parking lot to find a potty place. Walter wagging in the lead, Jack dragging in the back, his little legs trying to keep up, but we managed.

When we arrived in Kentucky, Walter was like an oversized three year old kid at Christmas. He was so amazed at the land mass he could run on, the horses and cows he had never seen before. He has new friends that welcomed him into their pack, and the pond/dog pool. I knew this was going to work. I still had no idea how much in love I would be with this dog.

Every day this big meat-headed dog stands at the door waiting for me to get home. The expressions he makes with his face are priceless. You can see him smile and you can see when he knows he should not have knocked over a glass with his big wiggly butt. He is my personal "fur-nace"—he sleeps with me every night. I even had to get a bigger bed! And he has to be by my side in what used to be my recliner. It is now his but I am a welcomed guest.

He is a celebrity in town. This Yankee was not liked just for being a Northerner when I moved here. For five years I had to stand my ground, but Walter? In five months he had a fan club. If I go into town no one asks me how I am doing, but they ask me, "Where's Walter?" Those who may not know me know my Walter. They love watching his big head stick out of the sunroof like a giant hood ornament as we cruise through the square (yes - it is a bit "Mayberry"), or having him shake hands on Sunday before Church. The best was when two elderly ladies saw him in my vehicle and asked to pet him. "We love pits," they said, "and they have such an unfair reputation."

These women were well dressed for church and over seventy years old and yet, they knew of the bad rap pits get. Walter got out of the Jeep and gave them each a big old hug and wet kiss. (Yes, he is a hugger—adults only though because he is so big). They had earned it just for recognizing and making such a heartfelt statement. Every day I get a gift. The gift of love and comedy from this big ninety-two pound, dorky lunk-head that snores like a bear, greets everyone with affection (even kittens) and drools over a pizza crust. I am forever grateful for the person who abandoned him because we found each other through Sheryl, the animal control officer, to whom my gratitude far exceeds words.

As for Rupert, his story is a bit different. Rupert's owner fell on some very hard times and was unable to keep him, but was terrified that he would fall into the wrong hands. Rupert unfortunately was with an owner who meant well and tried her best, but did not provide the right stimulation and environment for him. His previous owner did not socialize him with other dogs so he was aggressive towards them. This fact I was made aware of after committing to the project. He had also been served beer regularly by the previous owner's ex companion, which I found out when he happily jumped my neighbor for the empty beer can in his hand.

I also got a clearer picture by connecting the dots when questioning the previous owner about some of the behavior I had seen.

Rupert did have his own cat though, and apparently liked to play dress up. He loves people and cats. He is a very small registered pit at only fifty pounds. Sheryl understood the previous owner's situation and contacted me wanting to know if I could help out. As always, the Shelton Pound was almost at capacity and Rupert deserved a chance.

Now, how would I transport him the nine hundred and sixty-seven miles to my place? Through Facebook. I contacted a friend at the Humane Society in Bowling Green, Kentucky who happens to transport to the Northeast for them once a month, to give the dogs more adoption opportunity and to allow Bowling Green to remain one of the very few no kill shelters in Kentucky. The transport goes as far as Allentown/Harrisburg, Pennsylvania and was gracious enough to get Rupert from that point, allowing him to hitch a ride back to me. The previous owner arranged for him to get to Harrisburg and meet up with the transport. So at 2:00 a.m. on the Sunday before Thanksgiving, Rupert arrived in Bowling Green, Kentucky, and we were on our way to his new home.

He arrived for his first Thanksgiving turkey, which all dogs get at my place. "What a cutie, quite pretty, and a small guy," I thought. He was very sweet to people, loved to snuggle, and I thought he probably would not be too bad with other dogs. Well in the beginning, he was not socialized, but he is learning that I am the alpha of the pack. We have small missteps here and there, but his desire to be part of the group helps him every day.

In less than a month he can lie down and watch TV, (which is pretty funny because he has a fondness for animal shows and the nightly news) with three or four other dogs and not feel the need to dominate. He was just misunderstood—all too common with mismatched breeds and owners. We work on his training and manners each day. With structure Rupert is going to be a fitting member of the group, breaking his bad habits, enjoying his life here and most of all being safe.

CHEWY

THANKS TO LAURA BOOTH – SOUTHBARK RESCUE

I volunteer with a rescue organization in the Pensacola, FL area. In May, 2013, a three-month-old pit bull mix was turned in to our local kill shelter. A good samaritan found her dragging herself down a busy road. She had obviously been hit by a car.

Once the pup got to the shelter, our rescue was contacted and I volunteered to foster her. When she got to the veterinarian, x-rays showed both hips were fractured, her right back leg was also fractured and her front right leg was completely shattered. Pins were placed in her front leg due to the severity of the break. Two days after surgery, she came home with me.

I was worried about my cats, because of all that I had heard about pit bulls. I told my husband not to get attached. I told myself not to get attached. My husband and I were really not huge dog people, but this dog, that we named Chewy, stole our hearts. There has been no greater happiness in our lives.

When she got to our house, she could barely walk. I had to carry her to use the bathroom and around the house. We did physical therapy with her in our pool. By July, we knew her home was here with us. We had watched her grow from a scared, homeless puppy who was in pain all the time to a beautiful pit bull with the most loving heart I have ever known.

Since Chewy became a permanent resident in our home, I have had several other foster dogs and cats, including two kittens that were two weeks old. I was bottle feeding them in bed one evening and Chewy came up on the bed with me. She was so gentle with the babies, all she wanted to do was clean their ears! She has done this with all the puppies and kittens I have brought into the house. Today, her best friend is one of my cats.

Chewy has never displayed one iota of aggression towards any be-ing, animal or human. She greets everyone with a happy tail wag and big licks. She is my constant companion. Our attitudes have completely changed regarding pit bulls and the negativity sur-rounding them. I can now honestly say my life has been changed for the better, because of a pit bull!!

PART SIX

VOLUNTEERS

"Everybody can be great. Because anybody can serve. You don't have to have a college degree to serve. You don't have to make your subject and your verb agree to serve.... You don't have to know the second theory of thermodynamics in physics to serve. You only need a heart full of grace. A soul generated by love."

~Martin Luther King, Jr.

"I've seen and met angels wearing the disguise of ordinary people living ordinary lives."

~Tracy Chapman

ANGELS AMONG US
THE SHELTER VOLUNTEERS EVERYWHERE

I would like to take this opportunity to thank all of those who volunteer their time in shelters. These people walk the dogs, play with them, teach them manners and fall in love with them. They see them go home and, all too often, they sit with them in their final hours and see them take their last walks. Without the volunteers, many of these dogs would have no one. They are, in every way, angels on earth.

MANNY AND JADE

THANKS TO ELISA LAFONT – SHELTER VOLUNTEER, BROOKLYN, NY

MANNY

I have never really lived the phrase "being at the right place at the right time" until Tuesday, November 15, 2011. I was able to head over to the kennel where I volunteer, since I got out of work early. As usual, time started to fly as we were walking the dogs. We were on our last walk with two dogs as we approached the front end of the shelter. There stood a family waiting for someone to speak with them. It was a couple with their baby. They came in specifically looking for a pit bull.

The woman said she had been watching a lot of *Pit Bulls and Parolees* on television and that she had fallen in love with the breed. It is not every day you see a family looking for a pit bull, so this was actually a breath of fresh air. They wanted to know if we knew which dog would be right for them. My fellow volunteer, Mike, instantly said, "I have the perfect dog for you." By this time it was already past 7:00 p.m. so adoptions were closed, but we still did the meet and greet so they could come back the next day.

When Mike came back he had Manny with him. This dog may look intimidating to some, but in reality he was a total mush. He always walked side by side next to Mike and would not even give other dogs that barked at him the time of day. He just wanted to relax and take in any affection he was given.

The family started to interact with Manny and he loved every minute of it. The father, placing the baby on his knee, invited Manny to come closer. Manny very slowly approached the baby, smelled her and leaned his body into her as if to let her know he would not bring any harm. You could feel the connection with everyone there. They fell in love with Manny and said they would be back the next day.

The next day came and they had not returned as promised. I noticed that Manny was on the "To Be Destroyed" list. I instantly let Mike know and both of our hearts dropped into the pits our stomachs. We were scrambling to figure out how we were going to save Manny. All we could think of was to network him like crazy. Mike messaged and emailed every rescue he knew. He also reached out to friends. While he believed this family would come back, I did not share the same hope because sadly, that is the case most of the time. People say they will come back but they never do.

It was the end of the shift for us so we did not know Manny's fate until the next day. Mike went into the shelter and sent me a message that the family that was there on Tuesday came back for Manny on Thursday morning. I was ecstatic! They felt terrible about not coming back the very next day.

This just goes to show that you cannot waste any time, especially when it comes to saving a life. Had they not come back when they did, Manny might have been gone. All that matters, though, is that they did come back, and just in time for him. Mike helped get Manny safely loaded into the car and off he went to his new life.

Later that same night, Mike sent me this email from Manny's new mom. "I just took Manny for a walk and he lunged at two people and growled. Does this happen often?" My initial reply was, "Oh no." I had never seen anything like that from him before. Mike replied back to them and gave them his number in case they needed to talk. Shortly after that he received another email: "Hey, ok so my husband walked him and he was perfect. I guess for me it was too much too soon! He is so perfect! I cannot thank you enough. Here is a pic I just took in his new bed." Mike and I both heaved a sigh of relief.

A few days later, Mike emailed the family to follow up and make sure all was going well. This was the mom's reply:

"Hey! He is great! A total mush!! I have such an amazing connection with him I cannot even explain! I've noticed that when I walk him alone and someone comes near me he jumps and barks at them, but when someone else walks him or I am accompanied by others, he does not even acknowledge them. Haha! I guess he is just protecting his mommy! And he loves his toys! Also, his cough is getting a lot better! We will keep you updated! Expect a holiday card at the shelter! Talk to you soon!"

When I read this, it just hit me so hard for some reason. That Manny loves his family so much and knows instinctively who to protect is amazing. I guess that first night he was just protecting his new mommy.

It is truly amazing how things turn out sometimes. Had Mike not been there when that family came, Manny might be dead right now. They would not have been allowed into adoptions past 7:00 p.m. They would not have known how gentle and perfect Manny was if it were not for Mike. This could not have turned out any better. This story will stay with me forever and I am glad to be a little part of it, but really, Mike did all the work.

JADE

Jade is the first project I took on when I began as a volunteer at the Brooklyn shelter. When I met her she was terrified of everything. There was just something about how she would look at me that made me want to invest all I had in her. I spent hours working with her, trying to make sure a family would see her as the loving dog I knew she would be, once she felt safe.

I went after work one night to focus solely on her. I had her out for an hour or so. When I was walking her back to adoptions, I saw a mother and her two children leaving and they noticed Jade. I asked them if they had found a dog and they said that they had not. I told them Jade was far less fearful than when she arrived, but that she would need a patient family to build her confidence back up and make her realize that no one would hurt her again. They fell in love with her and said they would be back the next day, since it was already 7:00 p.m. and the shelter was closing. They did indeed come back and adopt her!

Fast forward about a year and a half. I saw another volunteer walking a dog that looked exactly like Jade. I said, "Wow that dog looks just like Jade except much happier and very confident." I checked her kennel card and sure enough it was Jade! I was so sad, but so happy to see her. I found out the owner got very sick and could no longer care for her, but I could tell the family did an amazing job with her. They were devastated when they had to bring her back.

I then reached out to my rescue friends as soon as I realized it was my Jade and the first dog I ever helped to get adopted. A Darrah Bull Bully Rescue pulled her as soon as they could. She was out of the shelter before she could even get sick. I was beyond thrilled and appreciated it beyond words. They all fell in love with her at the rescue. Jade found her forever home shortly thereafter. She has a human baby sister. They are the best of friends.

For shelter volunteers, there are many dogs that come in and out of our lives but there are some that touch our hearts more than others. Whenever I see a new picture of Jade, I am reduced to tears. To think, they would have likely killed Jade because of her fear. You never know how much a little bit of work can change a life.

SWEETPEA, FIONA AND BRIDGET BARDOT

THANKS TO JACKIE SEAL – SHELTER VOLUNTEER, TAMPA, FL

I hope you are being inundated with stories and, if that is the case, then please disregard mine as I have not actually rescued a pit bull, so am no doubt disqualified! I do, however, volunteer at two rescue shelters here in Tampa and for what it is worth, I have only positive things to say about every pittie I have ever met. In fact, we who fall in love with pit bulls don't just love them, we are passionate about them.

My first story is about a dog I ended up calling Sweetpea. I was putting gas in my car at my usual gas station opposite Busch Gardens, on a very busy street, and saw a female red-nosed pit bull just hanging around. She walked by me and stopped for me to pet her, before making the rounds to other customers. By the time I finished filling my tank, she was right by my side again. I simply opened the door to the rear of my car and in she jumped, seemingly happy to be there!

I drove up and down the streets behind the gas station, asking people if they knew this girl, but no one did. She had no collar or tag, so I took her to the closest vet to be scanned for a microchip, but she had none. It was a Monday in December, the county animal shelter was closed on Mondays and the weather forecast for that night was for below-freezing temperatures.

I phoned my husband as I neared the house and asked him to bring our dog out on a leash to the front yard, neutral territory, so the two dogs could meet. Both tails wagged profusely, so we let them in the back yard together, where they played beautifully. We kept Sweetpea overnight and her behavior was impeccable. She was very sweet-natured and had obviously been well taken care of, which was why I very reluctantly took her to the animal shelter the following morning. I felt certain someone would be looking for her. All the same, I regretted not keeping her and praying she found her way home.

The second dog was Fiona. At the county shelter I walk dogs from one of the kennels that do not have outside runs, because the dogs really do need to get out. When I finish taking those dogs out, I walk through the facility and always take out one last dog that otherwise might be left alone. There are just too many of them for the volunteers to take out individually. Fiona was listed as being five years old and had been brought in as a stray. She was pitifully thin with her ribs and hip bones showing, and had Mange on her back, in other words, she was a dog most would consider to be totally unadoptable.

Off we went to the play yard. I had my camera with me, but it was difficult to take photos because all she wanted to do was put her front paws on my lap and be cuddled! She was so very happy, and so very sweet. I was leaving on vacation the following week so, once again, so I would not know what become of her after that. As with Sweetpea, at times we volunteers at kill shelters just feel it is better not to ask. We can pretty much guess what will happen, but confirmation of it would leave us in tears.

My last story is a happier one. I was looking for one last dog in the shelter's general population to take out before heading home. There was a very pretty black and white collie mix looking quite eager, but in the kennel next door was a large female brown and white pit bull showing signs of being overbred. She was about five years old and had been brought in as a stray. Someone had given her the name Bridget Bardot, which hardly suited her! I spoke to her and she lifted her head as if to say, "Why are you bothering with me, a big old ugly pit bull, when there are so many pretty dogs around?"

I went into her run and offered her a piece of hot dog if she would let me put my leash on her. Hot dogs work wonders! I knew instinctively she would be a sweetheart on the leash, and she willingly and very calmly came out with me to the play yard. She was happy and loving. It was as if nothing so wonderful had ever happened to her before, so we stayed out there together for a long time.

It broke my heart to put her back, but lo and behold a couple of days later, someone who posts shelter dogs' photos on Facebook must have seen in her what I saw, and posted Bridget Bardot's photo. Her photo was given wide distribution and finally a pit bull rescue took her in. Within two weeks she was adopted by a couple that already had a male pit bull. I was ecstatic!

If I ever have the chance to get another dog, it will definitely be a pit bull, and to everyone who says to me that pit bulls are vicious and dangerous, I always ask if they have ever met one personally, or ever gotten to know one. Not surprisingly, the answer is always no. Fortunately, our county shelter has a special pit bull program that is very successful. I am happy to say there are also quite a few pit bull rescue groups in the area. We all work together to restore the good reputations of these incredible dogs and offer them a brighter future.

LILY AND LACY

THANKS TO KIMBERLY BRODASKY – SHELTER
VOLUNTEER, WATERFORD, CT

I am the proud Mama of two rescued pit bulls, Lilith Fair, a.k.a. Lily, my blue nose, and Lacy, a.k.a. Pooter, my little red nose. I adopted Lily on September 11, 2011 and Lacy on January 23, 2012. They both came with sad pasts, which in some ways we are still overcoming, but are both spoiled rotten now.

Lily came from the Haddam, CT pound where my friend volunteered. She called my cousin and me, thinking we might be a good fit, and said we really needed to meet this dog. So we immediately drove to the shelter to meet her. In walked my Lil, formerly named Milley. She was originally given this name because of the way she was found.

Ok, now on to her story. It was the hottest day in August of 2011, and she was left outside in a crate full of feces. It was obvious that days earlier she had delivered puppies. She would not have been found if it were not for a dog named Tilley. Lily was abandoned at the far corner of a parking lot where no one would even know she was there. Tilley barked her head off until my Lily was noticed. Lily was very sick with untreated Lyme disease and many infections. She is on prednisone three times a week to this day due to a severe auto-immune problem.

Lacy came from the Waterford, CT shelter, where I was a volunteer. I fell in love with her instantly. She was a two-time loser at the shelter, meaning she was brought back twice for aggression issues, and was almost put down. Lacy is terrified of men and anyone who smells like alcohol or is drinking. It took a long time to figure out that it was these things that were high behavioral triggers, but my best guess is that she was beaten by someone, most likely male, who drank alcohol. She is still afraid and looks to Lily to be her Mama and best friend. They are inseparable.

RILEY JAMES AND TEAGAN

THANKS TO TAMMY PROP – SHELTER VOLUNTEER, HARVEST HILLS ANIMAL SHELTER, FREYBURG, ME

In 2010, I was volunteering at the Harvest Hills Animal Shelter in Fryeburg, Maine, when the Animal Control Officer came in with a white and black pit bull. The officer said a man had called about a dog in his garage going through trashcans, looking for food. He was picked up and brought into the shelter. Once there, the staff gave him the name Ringo.

A few days later I was walking through and I met Ringo. At first he was barking along with all the other dogs. I knelt down in front of his cage, our eyes met and I knew I had to adopt him. I told him out loud, "You are going to be my best friend and I will take care of you for the rest of your life."

I filled out the application and about a week later, he came home with me. He was so overjoyed that once in the house, he jumped from couch to couch without ever touching the floor. He knew he was home. In his shelter picture he looked so valiant and regal. I had to give him a fitting Irish name. His name would be Riley, which means "valiant one" in Gaelic. His middle name, James, came shortly after. I took Riley James to obedience training right away, had him micro-chipped and made sure he got plenty of socialization.

Now, let us fast forward to 2013. My husband Steve loves photography and was always taking pictures of Riley on top of his 18-wheeler. Riley loves the camera! I sent in one of his pictures to RoadKing magazine, along with a story about Riley going into a truck stop shower in Tennessee because my husband's air conditioning unit broke when it was about 100 degrees outside. RoadKing decided to put Riley on a magazine cover! The magazine even sent a photographer out to do a photo shoot.

I cried when I heard this because this dog came from eating garbage and sitting behind bars like a criminal to now living the life of well, riley! He always appreciates what he has and is so well behaved and loving that I wanted to share him with everyone. Now I was able to share him with a national magazine.

He may not have a Facebook page with a following of people and he may not have a horrifying past, but he has a normal life with normal people—except, he does have a magazine cover and he has my heart forever.

The other dog we have is a Craigslist survivor. Her name is Teagan and she is Riley's love! My husband found her in Indiana while he was trucking through. He saw her advertised on Craigslist. She was a female, not spayed, part pit bull and being sold very cheaply. He knew what would happen to her if she got into the wrong hands, so he adopted her. She is amazing.

JASMINE

THANKS TO SUSAN SCHIAVONE – SHELTER VOLUNTEER -
DANBURY DOG POUND, DANBURY, CT

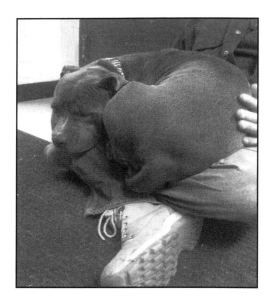

I volunteer at the Danbury Dog Pound. Jasmine is one of the dogs I walked and loved at the pound.

At any given time we have fifteen or so dogs that live in cages all week, with no access to walking, although they are otherwise treated very well. Most of the dogs have lived here far too long.

One day when I arrived at the shelter to walk Jasmine, she was not there—she had been adopted! I was thrilled to hear that a wonderful man came in to see her and adopted her on the spot. Look what she did when she met him. I wish I had been there to see her crawl right into his lap.

SKYE

THANKS TO MICHELLE CULHANE – SHELTER
VOLUNTEER, WEST COLUMBIA GORGE HUMANE
SOCIETY, WASHUGAL, WA

At three months of age, Skye (then called Nina) was tied up in front of the Spokane Humane Society in Washington, covered in Demodex mange. She was rehabilitated there and was adopted.

She spent a couple of years in a home with other pets and kids until they decided that they no longer wanted a big dog in the house. At that point she was returned to the Humane Society. She had horrible shelter shock and was deemed unadoptable, but she was a volunteer and staff favorite. The volunteers made videos and posted them on YouTube to help her find a home.

After five months in Spokane, she was transferred to the shelter where I volunteer, in West Columbia Gorge Humane Society in Washougal, WA. The Assistant Manager in Spokane thought so highly of her she drove five hours each way to get her to us.

She came in on a Thursday, was my foster by Sunday. By the next Wednesday I had adopted her, renaming her Skye because I felt she had unlimited potential and is a perfect dog. She quickly completed an advanced obedience class and passed her AKC (American Kennel Club) Canine Good Citizen Certification test on her first try. Our trainer is High Expectations in Camas, WA.

I have only had her for five months!

Skye now is a dog temperament test dog for our shelter, any other shelter that needs her and our trainer's private clients.

Skye goes into schools, from pre-school and up to high school, to teach about rescue, shelters, how to safely approach a dog, safety around strange or loose dogs, etc. Her best audience is fourth graders! She does hands-on work, in addition to teaching what good dog body language looks like.

She is in a tricks class now and will continue to grow with us. She loves going to our beach house and running on the sand after Frisbees. She lives with three other dogs and my two sons, ages one and four.

JAKE (AND MORE)

THANKS TO BRENDA PANE – SHELTER VOLUNTEER, HAYWARD ANIMAL SHELTER, HAYWARD, CA

Jake is the dog on the right in the photo. He was my first foster dog. His journey to a new life began on October 6, 2012, when he was found as a stray and brought to the Hayward Animal Shelter, where I volunteer. He was estimated to be about one and a half years old. At first, he was just like any other dog to me, a sweet, cute pit bull in a sea of sweet, cute pit bulls. However, he was unhappier about being in his kennel than most dogs are. He would practically knock you over in a mad rush to get out of the kennel when you would open the door to walk him.

He would also bark and bounce off the walls of his kennel when he wanted to get someone's attention. Jake had multiple factors working against him. First, he was a pit bull. There are always a lot of them at the shelter and pit bulls have a bad reputation. Most people do not want to adopt them because they are afraid of them or do not want to deal with the stigma that comes with having a pit bull. Second, because he behaved so poorly in his kennel, he was intimidating and undesirable even to the people who were looking for a pit bull.

The first time I took Jake to Petsmart to show him for adoption, I was actually surprised by how well behaved he was. He was calm and polite and acted nothing like he did when he was in his kennel. Jake proved to be great with large and small dogs, and even passed a test with cats. He quickly became my favorite dog at the shelter, and I was determined to save him. I already have two large pit bull mixes that I adopted from our shelter, and could not realistically see bringing in a third one long-term, so adopting him was not an option.

When I took him to Petsmart on February 2, 2013, I was told that his time was up and he was going to be put to sleep the next day if he was not adopted. He did not get adopted that day, but there was someone who was very interested in him.

When I got back to the shelter, I told the supervisor about the person who was showing interest and asked if Jake could have one more week. She agreed, but unfortunately, Jake did not have a home by the end of the week. However, we had an adoption event at the shelter that day and found homes for seven dogs. This extra kennel space enabled Jake to have a little more time. I was happy he was given a chance, but I knew he was living on borrowed time.

On March 8, 2013, Jake's stress level became so high that the shelter supervisors made the difficult decision that he either needed to go to a foster home immediately or be put to sleep. By this time, I had spent about 30 hours with him one on one at adoption events and had also taken him for countless walks at the shelter. I could not let this great dog be put to sleep. I brought my dogs, Kaedin and Odie, to the shelter to make sure they would get along with Jake. After a short introduction, the three dogs were playing like they had known each other their whole lives. This made it easy for me to decide to foster Jake. He loved being at my house and was able to unwind quickly from the stress of the shelter.

My dogs helped him burn off months of pent up energy. He quickly learned how to use the dog door and was housetrained in just two days. I brushed his teeth, clipped his nails, gave him a bath, cleaned his ears, and restrained him while putting a bandage on his tail. He was so good – he allowed me to take toys out of his mouth and move him while he was sleeping. I trusted him completely.

On March 31, 2013, he was adopted. His new home did not have a yard or another dog for him to play with, but he was going to go for four walks a day and play with dogs at the park. Unfortunately, due to an unexpected job offer in another country, Jake was returned after only three days. I was heartbroken but Jake came back to my house with my dogs, they were happy to have their friend back. I figured that the only way this could be a positive thing would be if Jake found an even better home in the end.

That is exactly what happened about two weeks later. After nine adoption events at Petsmart, he finally found the perfect home. Jake's new dad, Justin, came in to look for a dog. He had a female pit bull that looked just like Jake and wanted to get her a friend. I told him how much Jake loves other dogs and showed him a picture of Jake asleep on the couch with my dogs. I also told him about all of the great personality traits I had seen while fostering him.

Justin returned that same day with his dog, Cali. As it turned out, he had also adopted her from our shelter about a year earlier. The two dogs were instant friends. Soon after the adoption, Justin sent me pictures of Jake and Cali lounging on the couch and videos of them playing in the yard. He also brings the dogs to Petsmart to visit me once in a while.

During the remainder of 2013, I fostered and found homes for four more dogs that were scheduled to be euthanized due to lack of space at the shelter. Three of them were male pit bull mixes, just like Jake. My dogs are both males too, which pretty much dispels the myth that you should not have male dogs together. As long as they are all neutered and the dogs are introduced and managed properly, gender should not matter. It was definitely strange to have my fifth foster be a female shepherd mix after all of the male pit bulls, but my dogs did not discriminate!

Jake paved the way for other foster dogs, and I continue to follow the same routine each time I bring a new one home. Once they are comfortable I am able to get some great pictures of the foster dogs playing and sleeping with my dogs to post at the shelter and bring to Petsmart. I also post pictures and videos of them on the shelter's Facebook page. The extra knowledge I can give potential adopters after living with a dog, even if it has only been for a few days, is priceless in helping people to decide if it is the right dog for them. My dogs are invaluable in helping me train and socialize the foster dogs. I gave my dogs a second chance in life, and I believe that they are paying it forward to each foster dog that walks through the door. I know there are going to be many more for us in the future!

PART SEVEN

SAYING GOODBYE

"How lucky I am to have something that makes saying goodbye so hard."

~ Winnie the Pooh

"The reason it hurts so much to separate is because our souls are connected. Maybe they always have been and will be. Maybe we've lived a thousand lives before this one and in each of them we've found each other. And maybe each time, we've been forced apart for the same reasons. That means that this goodbye is both a goodbye for the past ten thousand years and a prelude to what will come."

~Nicholas Sparks

PETUNIA

THANKS TO JENNIFER COOLEY

I have always been an animal person but one animal in particular changed me.

My husband and I were talking about getting a dog when we first married in 2004. He went to the Humane Society one day and found a dog that he wanted. We went back the next day and when the dog came out I was less than impressed. She was a light gray colored pit bull and was running around the small area in the back of the shelter like a wild animal.

I did not immediately have a connection with this dog at all. Of course at the time, I had not understood that this was probably the first time she had been let out all day. Still, I was thinking that she looked mean and, like everyone else, I had heard the horror stories splashed over the media about pit bulls. Somehow, I agreed to take her home because my husband wanted her so badly. I insisted on naming her Petunia because I felt she needed a name that would draw attention away from her scary appearance.

Once she was in a normal environment, this wild dog calmed right down and I fell in love. It turned out she was the sweetest, most loving dog I had ever come across. Having grown up with lots of great dogs including Shelties and Cocker Spaniels, I was shocked that this big mean looking beast was so affectionate and so thankful to be loved.

Unfortunately, we came to understand that Petunia was formerly a bait dog, which means in dog-fighting circles she was dog that the other dogs practiced on. We noticed that she was not great with other dogs and sometimes aggressive, especially when food was involved since she was probably starved in her former life.

At the time, I was 24 and had moved into a home that we could barely furnish let alone make allowances for a fence to be put up. My husband and his family said we had to take her back because without a fenced in yard she was a liability to us. I was torn apart. In just a few months I had come to love this dog so much and the thought of taking her back broke my heart. Finally, I gave in.

Hindsight is always 20/20. I wish we had hired a trainer and tried harder to fix this one behavior. I wish we had the resources at the time to put up a fence. I wish I had the confidence to stand up to a family that said she was a liability. She had been trained by some evil monster to be aggressive toward other dogs so she very well could have been untrained.

I called the Humane Society every day asking if Petunia had been adopted, hoping and praying she had found someone that would give her the second chance she deserved. I went and visited her and cried my eyes out every time I saw her in there. Finally, one day, about six months later, I called and received happy news that she had been adopted by a couple with a fenced yard. I even went in to see the evidence that she had actually been adopted. Sure enough, there she was in a picture with her new family.

At 32 years old, I can say that Petunia, in the short few months I had the honor of knowing her, impacted my life more than anything else ever has. I am now a pit bull advocate, rescue advocate, volunteer dog transporter and owner of two rescue dogs. Both are eight years old now and although they are not pit bulls, they have Petunia to thank for paving the way into my heart.

Recently, I decided not to sign a lease for an apartment simply because there were pit bull breed restrictions. The fact that I do not currently have a pit bull is irrelevant, as I definitely plan on having one again someday. When that day arrives, I will be ready!

MYSTIQUE

THANKS TO DEAN FIORA

From 2004 through 2008, I lived with a roommate who had a pit bull mix. Somehow, Mystique never got the message that her breed was supposed to be vicious and violent. The most aggressive thing she would do is lick your face until it needed washing!

Mystique adored people, especially those who shared her living space. It was always a joy to get home, only to find Mystique waiting for me at the door and bouncing up and down as she tried to jump on me. If my roommate went out and I was in my bedroom with the door closed, Mystique would perch herself outside, whimpering up a storm and scratching at the doorjamb until I let her in.

I often took her for walks around the University of Connecticut campus. The students loved to pet Mystique, who was always happy to let them do so. A lot of those kids were hundreds of miles from home and undoubtedly missed the family dog, so Mystique would fill the void for the minute or two that a student bonded with her.

Unfortunately, I have not seen Mystique since I moved in 2008, but hardly a day goes by that she is not in my heart and thoughts. She always makes me smile just thinking about her!

DOLLY

THANKS TO JILL JACOBY

My fight to change the perception of pit bulls started with one sentence. "Here, no one wants her, they have little kids so she is yours." I already had a nice, comfortable life with two dogs that adored each other. This was a puppy and she was part pit bull but I did not have the heart to say no. Well, here we are about twelve years later and I am preparing to say goodbye to my best friend.

To say I love this dog sounds so trivial. About five years ago I was diagnosed with early stage cancer. Dolly was not so lucky when she was diagnosed with the same cancer soon after. I had surgery but she had two surgeries and six months of chemotherapy. My girl was a trouper and never missed a beat! She ran into the clinic every other week like she was invited to a steak dinner.

Recently I took in two pit bulls as a foster for the local shelter. They were on the euthanasia list and the volunteers reached out to me as a last resort. A few days after Zoey and Anna Lise came into my life, I noticed a lump on Dolly in that familiar spot that I avoided looking at previously.

There will be no surgery or chemotherapy for my girl this time. I will cherish every day we have left together and know that life will not be the same when she is gone. I have had many people tell me "you need to get rid of her, she is ruining your life." I have lost friendships and relationships, but I never, for one second considered that option. Dolly will be my girl until the end.

BROOKLYN

THANKS TO ROBIN RANDELL

This story is about my sweet girl, Brooklyn. My friend networks to save pit bulls. She would always beg me to foster a pit, but my answer was always no. The main reason is that I am not a well woman. I have back problems that at times, keep me bedridden. I was always afraid a pit would just be too strong for a woman in my condition.

One day I was on Facebook looking at pictures of dogs in the New York shelters. I saw Brooklyn with her ears back and her tongue sticking out. She was beautiful. I went into her profile and there was another picture of her smiling. I knew right there before even reading her profile that I had to save this girl. I called my friend Jen and she set everything up. The next day we both went to get her. We drove from Pennsylvania to New York.

From the moment my arms were around her I loved her. She was to be put down the next day, so we saved her just in time. The best part is that she was there longer than they normally keep dogs–I always felt like she waited for me.

She was so thin I could see all of her ribs, but in time she filled out. We bonded right away. From the first day it seemed that she knew of my problems and never was she rough with me. She would play rough with my son and others who were able to handle her but when I took her for walks she was always calm and by my side. There were times I could not even get out of bed to let her out, and interestingly, she never cried to go out.

She would just lay next to me as if to say, "It is okay mom, I'm here for you." I want to think that was her way of thanking me for saving her, although sometimes I think it was the other way around—she saved me. She gave me a reason to wake up every day. Our love grew more and more over the last three years. You see, I started out as her foster mom but fell in love and became her Mommy.

But there is a sad side to my story, more for me than for Brooklyn. Because of my back issues I could not work and became permanently disabled. I could no longer continue living where I was in Pennsylvania, and was forced to move to Colorado near my daughter. The housing I had to move into made no accommodations for dogs. I tried to find Brooklyn a good home in Pennsylvania but I was unable to, so when I packed up the car to drive to Colorado, guess who took a road trip across the country with me?

My daughter was none too pleased but I told her that I had not saved this dog from a shelter just to have her wind up back there. So when I got to Colorado, I stayed with my daughter for a few weeks until I could find a good, permanent home for Brooklyn. Mission accomplished!

Today she lives with a family with two other small dogs. The oldest son wanted a dog that he could go running and climbing with. As much as I missed her, I was happy for Brooklyn because she needs to run, jump and climb and I was never going to be able to give her that. This family will give her the enjoyment she so deserves. I will never forget our three years together. I loved her like a child and now my child has left the nest.

8BALL

THANKS TO RACHEL LEE

Back in January of this year I was contacted via Facebook by a former coworker about a dog in need, asking if I could help. A friend of a friend of hers lived next door to (and was actually the landlord of) a couple that had a male pit mix. Apparently the couple had marital difficulties and the wife moved out. As a result this sweet boy, who was once let indoors and played with the children, through no fault of his own, was now left outside, tied up 24/7 and basically neglected to the point that the landlord was coming over and feeding him.

The "owner" no longer wanted him and was going to take him to the pound. He was a pit bull and black so I knew he automatically had two strikes against him, so when I met him, something in his eyes just told me I could not leave him. On my birthday (February 1), I took this sweet boy home, vetted him and had him neutered out of my own pocket.

Since I already had four dogs of my own I knew I could not keep this sweet boy and give him the time he deserved. So I began the search for a new home for him. I found it in a young couple that already had a female pit bull puppy and were looking for a play-mate for her. In March, I placed him in what I thought would be a loving, forever home.

November rolled around. On the eighth, I was home on my day off and opened my email to find one from an unknown person with the subject heading, "Did you rescue 8ball?" Strange name, I know, but it is the one he came with. I read on and discovered that he had been dumped at the pound by the woman I had entrusted him to. Turns out, she and her husband split up, so now sweet 8ball was the innocent victim of another divorce.

I panicked, having no plan of how to fix this. I was already foster-ing another dog in addition to my own, but I knew I could not leave him there. He had already been there two weeks so I knew his days were numbered. I drove there as soon as I could and res-cued my sweet, loving boy once again. I took him home and it was like he had never left. He loves everybody! He is so forgiving, de-spite all he has been through in his short life. Oh, did I mention he had been shot as a puppy by an angry neighbor and lost a claw on a back foot as a result?

So now I needed to find a home for 8ball once again. But this time it had to be the perfect home.

Some friends of mine who had lost their pit mix earlier in the year missed having a dog in the house and were interested in 8ball. He seemed to be a perfect mixture of their previous two dogs. The only hitch was they now had an 18-month-old toddler and I was unsure if he had ever been around such a small child. So I took him over to meet her and it worked out wonderfully. Little Emily loves dogs (or dawg as she calls him) and he loves her. They even shared a drink from her sippy cup!

Now I am secure in knowing this amazing dog that I adore, has finally found the loving home he deserves and will live the rest of his days there with love and safety. The best part is they are only a few miles from me so I will still get to see him regularly!

ROCKY

THANKS TO SYLVIA ELIE

I used to have a pit bull named Rocky. My son found him behind a dumpster at Home Depot when he was about three months old. When my son came home with him I was totally against it for two reasons: I live in a complex that does not allow dogs, and he was a pit bull.

He was with us for nine months and he completely changed my perception of the breed. I have always had dogs and Rocky was the most affectionate, silly, beautiful, loving dog that I have ever had. When he was little he would sit on my husband's lap (he was maybe twenty or thirty pounds then). Fast forward to fifty to sixty pounds and he would still want to go on my husband's lap. I would ask him for kisses and sure enough he would nudge my cheek.

He was exceptional with my granddaughter. It was as if he knew she was smaller and he needed to be gentler with her. It is terrible that this breed is so discriminated against, all because some people have used these dogs for terrible things.

Unfortunately, I had to take him to Hi-Tor Shelter in Pomona, New York. I tried so hard to work with my management company so I could keep him. I went so far as to get a letter from my doctor stating that I needed to keep him as an emotional support dog. Management told me that it would be fine since I had a letter, but only if it was not a pit bull. It was clearly discrimination. Sadly, I was not in a position to move. To this day when I think of him, which is most days, I cry for him. He truly stole my heart. I am so happy that he was adopted from the shelter. A nice couple took him home.

People need to understand that any dog can be trained to be aggressive. It is all about how the dog is raised. As with humans, if you abuse someone and that is all they know, that will affect how they interact with others.

I wonder if people know that the pit bull was once considered the all-American dog. If I ever move from my present location and have the opportunity to again get a dog, I will definitely get a pit bull. It breaks my heart to see them in shelters.

A DOG'S LAST WILL & TESTAMENT

Before humans die, they write their last will and testament, giving their home and all they have to those they leave behind. If, with my paws, I could do the same, this is what I'd ask…

To a poor and lonely stray I'd give my happy home; my bowl and cozy bed, soft pillow and all my toys; the lap, which I loved so much; the hand that stroked my fur; and the sweet voice that spoke my name.

I'd will to the sad, scared shelter dog the place I had in my human's loving heart, of which there seemed no bounds.

So, when I die, please do not say, "I will never have a pet again, for the loss and the pain is more than I can stand."

Instead, go find an unloved dog, one whose life has held no joy or hope, and give my place to him.

This is the only thing I can give…

The love I left behind.

~ Unknown

DOZER AND ROCCO

THANKS TO DANA JONES

My husband and I had just rescued two mixed breed puppies when a red nosed pit bull puppy named Dozer also needed to be rescued. I had only one dog in my life, and she was thirteen and a Pomeranian. My husband brought Dozer home and even though I thought we were crazy, we kept him too. He wound up being my soul baby—he was the most gentle and sweet dog I have ever known. Do not get me wrong—he was a pit bull, could be stubborn and not listen at times, but he was never, ever, ever vicious. He was a great dog, who, at 80 pounds of solidness, wanted to be a lap dog. When I would cry he would come from anywhere, get up on my lap, and gently kiss my tears. He played hard and would get that beautiful pit smile that only a pit bull has.

At night, he was not happy unless he was sleeping in between me and my husband. He was the best dog ever. When he turned five though, he got cancer and we just could not save him. I lost my Dozer and it is a pain that, over two years later, still brings me to tears. I know he is waiting for me at the Rainbow Bridge. My husband and I were beyond broken, so nine days later we rescued Rocco, a white and brindle patched pit. He has so many of the same characteristics as Dozer, both so sweet and gentle. I love this breed and will always have at least one. People should know what wonderful dogs they are.

BELLA

THANKS TO FOSTER MOM KACI STOKLEY, SAFE HAVEN
ANIMAL CARE KENNELS AND SOUTH BARK RESCUE

Photo courtesy of Fox 10 News

Bella was rescued in February 2012, off of the chain, in McIntosh, Alabama where she existed for years—without food, water or adequate shelter. Bella crossed the rainbow bridge on Friday, December 14, 2012, as a direct result of the negligence she endured prior to her rescue.

She was rescued on February 14, 2012 by Safe Haven Animal Care Kennels (S.H.A.C.K.) and South Bark Rescue, and was brought to Ark Animal Clinic where she was treated for Sarcoptic mange and internal parasites. Upon further testing it was discovered that she had an advanced infestation of heartworms, a potentially fatal disease. Despite everyone's best efforts, Bella lost her battle only ten months after her rescue.

Let me give you some back story here. When I picked up Bella in March of 2012, we discovered she did not like other dogs, but I completely understood. I could only imagine how she was forced to defend herself on the end of that chain. Watching her discover and react to having a bed, regular meals, along with hugs and kisses, was unforgettable. She was still weak, but gaining weight and muscle in her back legs. For the first time in her life, she knew what it was like to be loved and cared for.

Bella learned that other dogs were not a threat to her any more, thanks to sessions with a local dog trainer. I watched her flourish from thirty-four pounds to a fifty-five, sometimes sixty pound, ball of thick fur, full of excitement and joy.

The heartworm disease was simply too much and she was suffering greatly. I lost one of my best friends, my kid, and my dog because she was so abused during her life on that chain. It has been brought to my attention that Bella's previous owner was charged with a misdemeanor in animal cruelty and his sentencing was forty-three days in jail and a one hundred dollar fine. He has not paid that fine and according to the authorities a warrant has been issued for his arrest.

I am appalled that such neglect and abuse resulted in such a minor penalty. Is that all that her life was worth? Is that what our government thinks is punishment for the torture and neglect that she endured by living her life on a chain, starving, without shelter, food, water, much less any medical attention? Her body was riddled with internal and external parasites and the government has the audacity to give him such a light slap on the wrist?

In Bella's honor I feel obligated, at the very least, to try creating some changes for the future of Alabama dogs. There are hundreds, even thousands more dogs just like Bella out there.

Bella got nine wonderful months in a home, and I am thankful beyond words that I had the blessing of having her in my life and being her mom, but there are many more that will never see that. They will never know a warm bed, a full belly, and plenty of water because the laws in Alabama allow them to live their lives at the end of a chain, starving and dying, and the owners are not fearful of the consequences because it is simply a slap on the wrist.

Please help us to help the abused, neglected, and forgotten dogs of Alabama and strengthen laws protecting them. Please be a voice for the voiceless. We must stand up and speak in order to make changes.

RUFUS

THANKS TO MARIE BRIGGS

Rufus was born on September 28, 2000, and came to live with me when he was six weeks old. I was in love with him the moment we met. He walked over, crawled into my lap, laid down and he had me. I adopted his sister Sienna, another pit bull puppy, in 2007.

Rufus was diagnosed with cancer back in January 2012—Multiple Myeloma. It is an uncommon cancer of the plasma cells—a kind of white blood cell that is present in the bone marrow. The doctor gave him 24 months at most. He underwent chemotherapy and back surgery and fought bravely. Rufus lost his battle in October 2013 and not a day goes by that I do not miss him.

I made a Facebook page, Rufus the Cancer Pitty, to have silly memories of him after he was diagnosed with cancer. The response was amazing. He had more than 8000 friends after one year on

Facebook. I was overwhelmed by how many people he touched and how much people loved him.

He may have passed on but he is still my most special boy. He was the most amazing, smart and loving pup I have ever met. I have had many people tell me that because of Rufus they were no longer scared of pit bulls. Some even adopted a pittie after learning about Rufus. He was also featured in American Dog magazine. I continue to update Rufus' Facebook page with photos of my girl Sienna in hopes that she can change minds too. https://www. facebook.com/RufusTheCancerPitty?fref=ts

LOUIE

THANKS TO SYLVIA WHITTUM

We lost our beloved pit bull Louie on June 19, 2008. Louie was 12 years old. He was a Humane Society rescue who came to us when he was a mere 6 weeks old. Louie was diagnosed with abdominal cancer in March of 2008.

Louie had always lived life at "full throttle." He seemed fine until early in March when he suddenly refused to eat and seemed in distress. We rushed him to the veterinarian (afraid of bloat). After a body scan, it was found that he had numerous cysts on top of a mass or tumor in the abdominal area. We hoped surgery would be an option, but the vet clinic felt that at his age it would not be in his best interest. We were told to bring him home, love him and enjoy him for whatever time he had left.

There was always the danger of the cysts bursting. Also the tumor began to grow, putting pressure on his lungs and his breathing was becoming labored. However, over the next several weeks Louie enjoyed playing, his walks and chasing squirrels. He was a fighter until the end.

Louie was a great dog who loved children and going into classrooms to teach them about humane education. He also loved other animals and joins his dear friends from his dog pack who have passed on before him. Louie was a treasured gift who will never be forgotten.

GENTLE GIANTS

THANKS TO NATASHA THOMPSON

My husband, son, and I had a pit bull and a Rottweiler for ten years. Sadly, we lost them both to old age a couple of years ago. This has left a hole in our family that has been difficult to manage.

My pit bull was wonderful with puppies and my son. He had a special ability to know exactly how much tug-of-war each one of us could handle. Our other dog and my husband would get into an all-out pulling match. He was far gentler with me. With my son he would just lay on the floor and shake his head a little and let my son do all the pulling (he was around six at the time).

He would also play with puppies at the dog park and would be gentle. He would even take the rope back up to them after he won and let them grab a hold, test it a little to make sure they had it, and then go again. It was amazing. Pit bulls are the most caring, loyal, and wonderful dogs you could have. And I love those pittie cuddles.

HUEY

THANKS TO CAROL DeMAIO

We adopted our first Pit in October 2000. My husband and I had decided to get a dog and wanted to save a life by adopting a rescue dog. I had done some research on shelters in our area and found a dog that was going to be at an Adopt-A-Thon at the Green in Norwalk, Connecticut. We went that day all excited to meet our possible new family member. Well, that shelter never showed up for the event. Sad but not quitting, we started to walk around to meet other dogs. I was a firm believer that our dog would pick us. We met many dogs but the spark just was not there.

Across the grass, I saw a dog being taken out of a car and wanted to go meet him. By the time I got there he was in a crate. I bent down and he seemed very excited to meet me. He was taken out of the crate and came right up to me for kisses. I knew then I wanted him to come home with us. I never asked what kind of dog he was—to be honest I thought he was a boxer mix since he had such a big blocky head.

We had to wait twenty four hours before taking him home, so we spent the rest of the day with him until he had to leave. He was rescued from the Bridgeport pound after he was found tied to a tree, starving. He was subsequently adopted but subsequently returned because he snored. He was rescued the second time on the day he was to be put down.

We went straight to PetSmart when we left to get all of the items we would need—a leash, bowls, a crate and food. We were so excited that we arrived to pick him up three hours before we were told to be there. There was a lot of paperwork for us to sign. As I started reading, I came to a section that said I confirmed that I lived in a town that did not have a pit bull ban and that I did own my home so a pit bull would be okay. I asked why that was in there and was told that since the dog is a pit, they wanted to make sure all conditions were met by law.

My heart skipped a beat. A pit bull? I called my husband over and showed him the paperwork because I was concerned. We discussed it and decided that we still wanted him despite his breed. He had many scars, which we later assumed were from being used as a bait dog for fighting. Due to where he was found and the fact that he was left to die. He apparently was not a good dog for fighting. He had such a wonderful heart. Despite all the abuse he had so obviously suffered at the hands of his humans, we had a loving, wonderful dog. I was nervous the first few days but the rest is history. He was with us until he was fifteen years old. Sadly, he got cancer and left us in 2012. We fell in love with the breed and have rescued our second pit.

Our experience with this breed has been wonderful and we have recently moved to Arizona. The first research I did was whether there were any breed specific bans. We are very lucky to now live in a town that accepts the breed and in fact, a lot of the shelters showcase some of their pitties for adoption. We love this wonderful breed, and take every opportunity to educate people on how loving and gentle they are.

SAMANTHA

THANKS TO DAWNMARIE SOUZA

In August 2000, I adopted a pit bull mix from The New Haven Animal Shelter. We guessed that she was about a year old, and was found tied to a fence in the rain, in the middle of the night. She had been beaten and starved. One look into her eyes and I knew she was my baby.

The shelter tried to give her to another person but I fought for her. I had just broken my arm at work and she knew instantly to be gentle with me. Amazingly, she was not food aggressive and my boys, then five and seven years old, could sit on her and she would almost purr–not growl but purr. She would sleep on my side of the bed when I was home and at the boys' bedroom door when I was working. She loved to play and go for car rides! She wore a seatbelt!

I had her for twelve years. The last four of which I had breast cancer. Samantha was 120 pounds but would tiptoe up on the bed to lay with me when I was sick. She would lie next to me on the floor when I vomited. I had no better companion. She became ill in 2011 and had to be put to rest February 23, 2012. She is resting on my mantle now. No one has ever experienced love and devotion like I had with her. She was truly the best dog ever.

CHEYENNE

THANKS TO VALERIE WOOLEY

One night, my red nosed pit bull Cheyenne, would not stop barking so I got up to see why. When I looked in the backyard I saw Cheyenne was barking at an opossum that was in our tree. It just happened to have a bird nest with three baby birds in it! I had been observing the birds for days, as the babies could not fly yet.

Cheyenne ran and barked up the tree just as the opossum tried to snatch a baby bird and it fell to the grass! Cheyenne snatched up the baby bird! To my surprise, she was gently holding the whole bird in her mouth and brought it to me! She opened her mouth and I retrieving the baby bird unharmed!

Cheyenne then climbed the wall and chased that opossum away! I quickly replaced the baby back in the nest where he stayed for about another week until I watched all three learn to fly!

Those baby birds owed their life to my sweet Cheyenne, the "ferocious pit bull" who never hurt a fly and saved three little birds. Cheyenne lived to be nine years old.

A life of loyalty, gentleness and sweetness I will never forget!

DOLLARBILL

THANKS TO ASHLEY

I lost my pit bull DollarBill July 8, 2013. DollarBill was thirteen years old and had a very hard life before I found him. I took DollarBill in when he was three years old. We found him in the crawl space of a house we were looking to buy. He had been left there to die. Immediately, I took him to a vet who wanted to euthanize him because of the state he was in. Because of his condition, he could not stand up in the crate, was nineteen pounds of skin and bones, could hardly bark, and was chewing his tail because he was hungry, but I wanted to do whatever we could to save him. We got him neutered, back to a healthy weight and worked to improve his socialization. Despite former hardships, he fit right in with our other three dogs.

When my husband and I split up I left the dogs with him because I felt he was more financially able to look after them. I was living at my parents' house on the couch when one day he just dumped the dogs on our doorstep. I took them all back, and with the help of my parents, transformed the basement into their playhouse.

In October 2011, DollarBill started to limp. I sold my TV and other possessions and borrowed money to pay for his care. The x-rays showed extensive hip dysphasia and you could see indentations that looked like tow chain marks (neighbors said that was the previous owner's tactics – to beat him with a tow chain). I was heartbroken and my vet gave me two choices: 1) do two surgeries-six months apart that would cut the ball of his hip off and fuse it back together, or 2) Canine Orthotics.

DollarBill was almost twelve years old so I decided to try Orthotics (which my great boyfriend, now my husband, said he would help me buy). We visited K9 Orthotics and were referred to Dartmouth Veterinary Hospital, where it was recommended that we try acupuncture. Miraculously, with acupuncture and exercises, soon he was standing again and taking a few steps again! In October 2012, though, he went downhill and we thought it was time to let him go, but another miracle happened and he improved. At that point, we decided to try a wheelchair because his back legs were losing muscle mass and he was struggling to get up. DollarBill had a hard time with the wheelchair and only used it three times.

My vet said we were on borrowed time but I did not give up. I stayed home and did hospice care. I took him in for vet treatments and check-ups more often. Started pain medication and helped him with everything he needed, including carrying him to use the bathroom and cooking all his foods at home.

But on July 6, 2013, I woke up and realized he was not happy and I was prolonging his suffering even though I was giving it my all to help him. I lost him the following Monday. I am still beyond heartbroken.

Now I just want to hold his memory high and show that a pit bull is a good dog. DollarBill was not just a dog, he was my family. We had him cremated and he sits on my nightstand so I can keep him close at night like I once did. He used to sleep beside me in bed on his very own pillow.

OWNING A PIT BULL –
WHAT YOU SHOULD KNOW

It has been said that pit bulls are too much dog for most people. They are special dogs that need special owners, but breed enthusiasts are adamant in saying that once you have owned a pit bull you will never want to be without one. Nothing compares to this breed.

As we have learned, however, for every pit bull that is adopted from a shelter, there are 600 that are not. This does not even take into account the pit bull deaths resulting from abuse, neglect and dog-fighting. This is unacceptable in a society that prides itself on freedom, compassion and justice. On the other hand, for every positive story, like the ones you have read here, there are thousands more like it, and I see this as a ray of hope.

I would like nothing more than to see every dog, regardless of breed, in a loving home. It may be a dream but I hope it will someday be a reality. For this to happen, though, there must be a crackdown on irresponsible breeders, puppy mills and even limits placed on the sale of puppies in pet stores. Stricter laws must be put into place and enforced in cases of animal cruelty, abuse and neglect. There must be incentives for people to spay and neuter their pets. People need to be made aware of the animals in shelters and rescues, and encouraged to adopt rather than purchase. If you do purchase from a breeder, be sure it is a reputable one. Avoid and report any that do not treat their dogs well, breed them to be aggressive or send them home before they are weaned.

Until there are no homeless dogs, we can all do our part to save one dog at a time, in whatever capacity we are able. Adoption is not an option for everyone, but if you are considering adopting a pit bull, it is important to do your homework.

While you may now have the urge to go out and save a pit bull, and I hope you will, you will first need to find out if the city or town in which you live has any type of Breed Specific Legislation.

> Breed-specific legislation (BSL) is the blanket term for laws that either regulate or ban certain breeds completely in the hopes of reducing dog attacks. Some city/municipal governments have enacted breed-specific laws. However, the problem of dangerous dogs will not be remedied by the "quick fix" of breed-specific laws—or, as they should truly be called, breed-discriminatory laws.

> It is worth noting that in some areas, regulated breeds include not just American Pit Bull Terriers, American Staffordshire Terriers, Staffordshire Bull Terriers, English Bull Terriers and Rottweilers, but also a variety of other dogs, including American Bulldogs, Mastiffs, Dalmatians, Chow Chows, German Shepherds, Doberman Pinschers, or any mix of these breeds—and dogs who simply resemble these breeds. (4)

Even if your community does not have such legislation, if you plan to travel with your pit bull you will need to research the laws in the cities and towns that you will be passing through. There have been instances where pit bulls have been confiscated from unknowing owners who simply stopped to walk their dogs.

It should be noted that Animal Welfare organizations universally oppose BSL as there is no real evidence that it is effective. It also does not take not account a dog's upbringing, personality or environment, and it punishes responsible dog owners. Still, it is a reality in certain areas and must be a consideration for anyone wishing to adopt a dog. The encouraging news is that animal advocates across the country have challenged these laws and, in many states, have succeeded in getting them replaced with laws that target the owners of dangerous dogs, regardless of breed.

You should also know the animal protection laws of your state. A study by the Animal Legal Defense Fund ranks the animal protection laws in various states from best to worst, with the top five being Illinois, Oregon, Michigan, Maine and California and the bottom five being Wyoming, New Mexico, South Dakota, Iowa and Kentucky. The results were based on the answers to 43 questions in 15 categories but did NOT rate how effectively the laws are enforced. (5) Research the laws that are currently on the books in your own state and also look at whether or not the current laws are being enforced.

If you own property, it is important to check your Homeowner's Insurance policy to make sure you are covered. Right or wrong, many companies will not insure homeowners who own certain breeds of dogs. Similarly, if you are a renter, be sure your lease allows pets and your landlord will allow you to own a pit bull. Again, even if the landlord does not have a problem with your dog, his insurance company may have a different view.

Before you adopt a pit bull, it is important to keep in mind that some of these dogs may have suffered unspeakable abuse. Even under the best of circumstances, they are stubborn, strong and willful. Their levels of aggression toward other dogs may be non-existent or severe, depending on the dogs' personalities and upbringing, although most are somewhere in the middle. Most shelters do behavior assessments. Read the shelter notes and take them seriously. Know what you are getting into.

On a positive note, pit bulls are highly intelligent and learn quickly. They love to play and may tolerate rough play with children like few other breeds. When properly socialized, they are more likely to shower humans with kisses than to attack. Pit bulls need owners who are strong physically and mentally. Pit bulls are typically affectionate and loyal and they are unconditionally devoted to their humans. As the owner you hold the key to your dog's success. It is a responsibility that must not be taken lightly, especially in a world where pit bulls already have two strikes against them.

For the most part, owning a pit bull is similar to owning any other breed. As with *any* dog, training and socialization are essential to your dog's health and well-being as well as your own. While it is important to encourage adoptions of pit bull type dogs from shelters and rescues to reduce the rates of euthanasia, the worst thing would be for your dog to wind up back in a shelter, or worse, because you were not prepared.

Any new dog requires at least a month to adjust to his or her new home and sometimes even longer in the case of shelter dogs. These dogs have been kept in cages with little or no exercise or human contact for days or weeks, sometimes even months or years. It can be stressful for them, whether they came from a home or were abandoned in the streets. Be prepared to give them time to decompress and learn what it is like to be part of a family. Don't expect miracles.

During the first few days, expect your dog to experience some stress and confusion. Give the dog time to acclimate to his or her new surroundings. Supervise all interactions with other family pets and make sure children know the proper way to approach a dog without frightening it. Do not introduce your new dog to strangers immediately. Do not force interactions with people or other dogs. Let your dog come to you or others on his own terms.

Find out what kind of food your dog is used to and continue with the same brand. If you decide to make a change, do so gradually, mixing some of the new food in with the old food for the first week or so. Have chew toys available and if you have other dogs, feed each dog separately or supervise them at mealtime.

Even if you are told your dog is housebroken, expect some accidents until he adjusts to his new environment. Take him to a spot outside where you want him to relieve himself and continue to do so until he knows what is expected. This is especially important after eating or drinking. If there is another dog in the home, your other dog can help your new dog learn the ropes.

Over the next few weeks, it is important to take your dog to the veterinarian for a general exam, shots, and heartworm medications and to be spayed or neutered if this has not already been done. There are now many low-cost clinics that make basic care and immunizations affordable for everyone. It is also a good idea to microchip your dog in case he becomes lost.

Begin a routine of daily exercise and play as soon as possible. Pit bulls are headstrong, they need consistent training and constant socialization. They need a lot of exercise and should never be left tethered or chained outside. All dogs are happiest with structure and routine.

If you notice any behavioral issues, contact a trainer immediately, and even if you don't, it is a good idea to enroll in a basic obedience class. This will strengthen the bond between you and your dog and also give your dog the opportunity to interact with people and other dogs in a controlled environment. Do not have unrealistic expectations. As with humans, no dog is perfect.

For first time dog owners, adopting an adult pit bull with an unknown past from a shelter may not be the best way to go. Actually, for those who are inexperienced, adopting any adult dog from a shelter may not be a good idea unless you are committed to proper training and socialization and are prepared to work hard with your dog to overcome any behavioral or emotional issues. Keep in mind that if the dog has been abused or is fearful for any reason, it may take years to rehabilitate and some dogs may never recover.

You might, instead, want to consider a pit bull puppy, but that will come with its own challenges. The first step is to puppy-proof your home. Similar to baby-proofing, you will need to cover electrical outlets, remove breakable objects, dangerous chemicals and houseplants. Use baby gates to limit access to stairs. Invest in an exercise pen for playtime in a confined space. Stock up on chew toys and larger balls. Sturdy toys are best. Avoid any toy that can be chewed into small pieces and swallowed. Most importantly, be sure to train and socialize your puppy from day one and continue throughout your dog's entire life.

Of course everyone loves puppies, but older pit bulls need homes even more, and there are some advantages to owning a more mature dog. Often they will already be house trained and will require a little less exercise and other training.

If a puppy is not for you, one option would be to adopt from a rescue rather than directly from a shelter. Dogs in rescue are generally placed with foster families and have lived in homes, often with children and other pets. They have already been temperament tested by people who do this for a living. They have usually been spayed or neutered and vaccinated. Many of these dogs have been family pets who were given up due to a change in circumstances and will make wonderful companions. Bear in mind though, that your rescue dog may have already been shuffled around and, as with any new dog, will require a period of adjustment. Many rescues will also take the dog back if things don't work out, although this is not encouraged.

Regardless of your dog's age, set consistent boundaries and enforce them for the life of your dog. Insist that your dog sit and wait for food or treats. Train your dog not to jump on people. This is especially important with a strong breed like the pit bull. Even if he just wants to play, he could knock someone over in his exuberance, resulting in serious injury. Have him sit and stay when you enter the house and be sure to go in first. When you leave the house for a walk, be the first to exit and have your dog follow you. When walking him on a leash, your dog should be next to you or slightly behind you. Your dog should never be allowed to walk ahead of you. With a pit bull as with any dog, it is important to establish yourself as the leader or "alpha" in the pack and always be consistent. There are many free resources and training videos available online and at your local library. Be sure to take advantage.

Pit bulls should be walked on strong leashes or, if necessary, owners should use a harness or special collar for greater control. Pit bulls love to be walked and love playing fetch and other games. Most enjoy swimming. Although they look intimidating, these dogs are extremely devoted. They can be a lot of fun and are easy to care for. They are hardy and require little grooming. Being a short-haired breed, pit bulls should never be left outside in cold temperatures. Your pit bull may enjoy the comfort of a coat or sweater for walks on cold days.

Finding a safe place to allow your dog to play off-leash can be a challenge. Some dog parks and day care facilities do not allow pit bulls at all. Even if you find one that does, be aware that not all dog owners properly socialize their dogs and, if trouble ensues, your dog, being a pit bull, could be unfairly blamed and even confiscated by Animal Control. It may be in your dog's best interest to invest in a fence for your yard or take him to play in areas where there are fewer dogs or where all dogs must be kept on leashes.

Always supervise your dog, regardless of breed around other dogs and children. Be in control of your dog at all times when out in public. If you own a pit bull, be prepared to go above and beyond the typical training knowing that people *will* find reasons to fault your dog's behaviors, even when it's not your dog's fault. For example, imagine another dog, let's say a Golden Retriever, attacks your pit bull and your dog fights back. Even if your dog isn't the instigator, and as unfair as it is, you will be blamed for the outcome.

Say you are a person who loves dogs but cannot adopt. Maybe you do not live in a pet friendly building, are prohibited from owning a pit bull or maybe you simply already have as many dogs as you can comfortably handle. You can still make a difference.

Here are some things you can do:

- Volunteer with a rescue or at your local shelter. Transport a rescue dog to a foster home or adoption event. Offer to do home checks for local rescues. Organize a collection drive or fundraising event. Walk, play with and help socialize the dogs in shelters or boarding kennels. Volunteer at adoption events. Offer to foster a dog, even if it is only short-term.

- If the animal abuse/neglect laws in your state are not strict enough, advocate for change.

- Join the fight against Breed Specific Legislation.

- Stop irresponsible breeding – push for spay/neuter requirements and adopt from shelters and rescues.

- Share photographs and biographies of shelter dogs on social media sites for increased exposure. Networking saves lives.

- Most importantly, if you see an injustice being done to an animal – report it! Call your local authorities. Take pictures. Keep documentation of all contacts and follow up with the appropriate investigating agencies.

Remember, owning a pet is a commitment for the life of your pet. Have a plan when you go on vacation and a place for your pets in case of an emergency. Responsible ownership is only the beginning. We must also be on the lookout for people who violate laws or otherwise mistreat their pets and take steps to ensure that it is not allowed to continue.

While owning any dog is a responsibility in itself, one big difference when your dog is a pit bull is that you will meet people who are afraid of your dog and for no good reason, only because of its breed. Instead of being upset, use it as an opportunity to educate. Once he is trained, take your pit bull out into the world. Talk to people, knowing that with each person you reach you are taking one small step toward changing perceptions. Education is the key to change.

It starts with each of us. We must always treat our pets with kindness and respect and ensure that others do the same. We must teach our dogs the rules of the society in which we live. We must protect them from harm. Together we can bring about changes. It all starts with us.

(4) http://www.aspca.org/fight-cruelty/dog-fighting/breed-specific-legislation

(5) http://aldf.org/wp-content/uploads/2013/12/2013-United-States-Animal-Protection-Laws-Rankings.pdf#!

AFTERWORD

"Here's to the crazy ones. The misfits. The rebels. The trouble-makers. The round heads in the square holes. The ones who see things differently. They're not fond of rules, and they have no respect for the status-quo. You can quote them, disagree with them, glorify, or vilify them. But the only thing you can't do is ignore them. Because they change things. They push the human race forward. And while some may see them as the crazy ones, we see genius. Because the people who are crazy enough to think they can change the world, are the ones who do."

~ Jack Kerouac

When I began this project, I had no idea where it would lead. I was not sure it would lead to anything at all. It started slowly, with a few stories sent to me by people I know and others I reached out to through mutual connections. At the time, I had no idea I would ever have enough material to write a book.

Once the emails began though, they poured in for days. Each story was a little different but the essence was the same. It was not only heartwarming but also humbling to read story after story, written by people who love their dogs. Whether or not the world is changing for pit bulls is debatable, but we who love them must never stop trying. I sincerely believe that together we can make a difference.

I thank all who took the time to speak with me in person and on the telephone and all who shared my idea and desire for stories within their own networks and on social media sites. Most of all, I thank the contributors, for not only taking the time to write and giving me permission to use their stories and pictures, but more than anything, for being brave enough and kind enough to love these dogs as they deserve to be loved. I hope I have delivered a quality product, worthy of your time, your effort and your devotion to your dogs.

I also wish to thank all of my friends in the rescue community, my family for supporting and encouraging me through this new and exciting venture, my life partner Matt, for putting up with me and finally seeing the light and adopting two unwanted dogs (one a pit bull), Dawn Harden of Floral Greens Publishing for her knowledge and expertise in publishing, copyediting, marketing, social media, website building and anything else I have needed, as well as all the hard work she has done and continues to do on my behalf, and Createspace for giving new writers like myself the opportunity to have our work published.

Finally, I wish to thank my son Aaron, a professional writer, for giving me the idea for this book and offering the benefit of his experience with writing and publishing, and my daughter Gloria, a digital media specialist for devoting countless hours to reading and editing my material and offering many helpful suggestions. To both of you, I feel truly blessed and proud to be your mom.

ABOUT ME

I have had several careers in my life, more out of necessity than of choice, and, while I enjoyed each one for different reasons, I was not truly passionate about any of them. I guess I am one of those people who always wondered what I wanted to do when I grew up. When I really thought about it, I realized I have only one passion. I am a dog lover. I always have been and always will be.

I have owned dogs all of my adult life. None of my dogs have been purebreds, none have been purchased from breeders or pet stores and all of them, I believe came into my life to teach me something. My journey with my first pit bull, Mickey, has taken many twists and turns and led me to some very unexpected places. It has not been easy but it has totally been worth it. I am grateful every day that he chose me as his mom.

My time now is devoted to saving dogs, especially dogs like Mickey, the abused, the lonely and the unwanted pit bulls that only need one person to believe in them and give them a chance. To all of those who help animals in need: the rescues, the volunteers and anyone who gives a lonely dog a home, I thank you from the bottom of my heart.

I finally know what I want to do now that I am grown up, and I am doing it. I am truly living the dream.

SOURCES

Websites

(1)   http://www.examiner.com/article/pit-bulls-and-euthanasia-rates

(2)   http://amhistory.si.edu/militaryhistory/collection/object.asp?ID=15

(3)   http://www.today.com/pet   shelter-dogs-caught-cuddling-are-adopted-after-outpouring-support-2D11644674

(4)   http://www.aspca.org/fight-cruelty/dog-fighting/breed-specific-legislation

(5)   http://aldf.org/wp-content/uploads/2013/12/2013-United-States-Animal-Protection-Laws-Rankings.pdf#!

(6)   http://www.pbrc.net/

(7)   http://www.badrap.org/

(8)   http://www.humanesociety.org/

(9)   http://shadylanefarm.us/

Books

The Dogs Who found Me: What I've Learned from Pets Who Were Left Behind - Ken Foster - Lyons Press (March 1, 2006)

The Lost Dogs: Michael Vick's Dogs and Their Tale of Rescue and Redemption – Jim Gorant - Gotham; Reprint edition (September 6, 2011)

The Pit Bull Placebo: The Media, Myths and Politics of Canine Aggression – Karen Delise - Anubis Publishing (June 11, 2007)

Pit Bulls For Dummies – D. Caroline Coile - For Dummies; 1 edition (March 28, 2001)

The Essential Pit Bull - Howell Book House; 1 edition (March 26, 1999)

Be the Pack Leader: Use Cesar's Way to Transform Your Dog... and Your Life – Cesar Milan and Melissa Jo Peltier - Harmony (September 23, 2008)

Film

"Beyond the Myth" – Libby Sherrill - Screen Media

ACKNOWLEDGEMENTS

Theodora DeBarbieri – The Examiner, Pound Posse Presents

Sherry DeGenova – Animal Control Officer City of Hartford

Carey Yaruss Sanders - Head Nurse/Assistant Manager: Bear Creek Veterinary Alternatives

Angela Hooker - Community Outreach Director Saving Grace, Inc.

Don and Sylvia Whittum – Shady Lane Farm

Nanette LaRochelle – Waggin' Train Rescue

Dawn Harden – Floral Greens Publishing LLC

18662205R00211

Made in the USA
Middletown, DE
16 March 2015